THE ADOLESCENT
AND HIS WORLD

Irene M. Josselyn, M.D.

FAMILY SERVICE ASSOCIATION OF AMERICA
44 East 23rd Street   New York, New York 10010

Copyright, 1952, by

FAMILY SERVICE ASSOCIATION OF AMERICA

All rights reserved. No part of this book may be reproduced without permission in writing from the publisher.

Fourteenth Printing, 1976

ISBN: 0–87304–019–8

Printed in U.S.A.

CONTENTS

	Page
Foreword.	3
Introduction.	5
I. Physical Aspects of Adolescence	9
II. Psychological Growth Patterns.	16
III. Social Pressures.	26
IV. Social Adaptation.	38
V. Dependency and Ambivalence.	47
VI. Psychosexual Conflicts	56
VII. The Fate of the Conscience.	67
VIII. Treatment Through Supportive Measures	76
IX. Psychiatric Treatment of the Adolescent	93
X. Sex Education and Sexual Behavior	109
XI. Conclusions	120
References	123

FOREWORD

The Family Service Association of America is greatly indebted to Dr. Josselyn, who undertook the preparation of this volume at the request of the Association. Because of the wide interest in her article, "Psychological Problems of the Adolescent," which appeared in *Social Casework* in May and June, 1951, the F.S.A.A. Publications Service suggested that she expand the subject for publication in this form. Most of the material is entirely new; in a few chapters, some of the formulations and illustrations presented in the original article have been incorporated.

This volume, as was her earlier one, *Psychosocial Development of Children,* is designed primarily for social workers and other professional persons who carry responsibility for helping to improve the interpersonal relationships of parents and children and who, through direct contact with adolescents, offer personal guidance and help in social planning. The technical focus of the material presupposes that the reader has considerable knowledge of dynamic psychology. A bibliography is appended, as an aid to further study of the subject.

It seems appropriate, in making this acknowledgment of the Association's debt to Dr. Josselyn, to comment on her many contributions to the field of social work. She has given generously of her time, serving as consultant to agencies, as a seminar leader, and as a participant in regional and national conferences. Her identification with the aims of social work and her belief in its therapeutic potentials are abundantly clear to all who work with her. In her writing, she has the gift of relating her technical knowledge to the concrete problems of day-by-day living. Her focus is always on the human being—not on abstractions. In this discussion, the bewildered and bewildering adolescent is her subject. In the course of describing the struggle of the young person

FOREWORD

in finding his adult moorings, Dr. Josselyn gives the reader a comprehensive outline of the psychological processes involved in the achievement of emotional maturity.

A word should be said about the appreciation that has been expressed for her earlier volume, *Psychosocial Development of Children*. It has had a wide distribution and is used extensively in schools of social work, seminars, and institutes, both in the United States and abroad. Dr. Josselyn has given permission for its translation and publication to two European schools of social work, one in the Netherlands and one in Austria.

It seems likely that this volume will be received with the same enthusiastic response.

CORA KASIUS, *Director and Editor*
Publications Service
Family Service Association of America

INTRODUCTION

Adolescence is frequently defined as the intermediate stage between childhood and adulthood. This definition, however, is not an entirely accurate one. It implies that childhood and adulthood are two sharply delineated periods of life, and that adolescence is a definite period that begins when childhood ends and is completed when adulthood is reached. In reality, the growth process does not occur in stages. Adulthood is the end result of gradual maturation that begins with the fusion of the ovum and sperm. Arbitrarily separating this process into periods gives the false impression that growth proceeds by "steps." Actually, the growth chart depicts a curve.

In the opinion of the writer, adolescence encompasses an extensive period of accelerated physical and psychological growth. Its onset can be determined by observation of physical changes. As will be indicated in the chapter on physical development, this period of change usually begins at about the age of ten in girls and the age of twelve in boys. Clinical evidence shows that modifications of the psychological structure take place at approximately the same time as the physical change occurs. The onset of the psychological changes is not so easily determined as the physical, partially because the changes take place more gradually but also because no accurate measuring techniques exist at present for determining changes in psychological growth patterns.

Adolescence terminates physically with the establishment of the mature body structure and the mature functioning of the glands of internal secretion, particularly those directly related to the reproductive system. It terminates psychologically with the establishment of relatively consistent patterns for dealing with the internal conflicts and the demands of reality experienced by the physically mature individual.

This broader concept of adolescence includes a younger age group than is usually placed in this category. Because of the importance of the early period of accelerated physical growth, the inclusion of this group seems valid. Some authorities divide adolescence into three periods: pre-adolescence, adolescence, and post-adolescence. Other writers refer to two periods: late latency and adolescence. Because physical development has such direct bearing upon the emotional aspects of adolescence, the writer prefers to include the period of rapid physical growth preceding puberty.

The correlation between the normal physical and normal psychological processes is perhaps more apparent in adolescence than at any other time. The effect on psychological adjustment of complications in the physical development and, in turn, the effect of psychological problems on physical well-being are familiar manifestations. If it were possible to create an optimum environment for an individual who has an optimum psychological and physical constitution, the correlation between physical and psychological growth would probably be more clearly demonstrable. Because both psychological and physical development are influenced by conditions of the environment as well as by the constitution of the individual, only a relative correlation can be made; a generalization about interrelationships between physical and emotional development does not necessarily apply directly to any individual case. By looking at the over-all picture of the individual's maturation process, however, rather than focusing on minute details, one may discern a definite pattern of correlation between the physical and emotional aspects.

An analysis of the interrelationships between physical and psychological growth can be approached from at least two different points of view. The adverse effects of failure to achieve normal growth in one sphere can be related to negative effects upon the other, or the constructive interrelationships can be correlated. The first category lends itself more easily to study. The effect of emotional disturbance on functioning of the body has been extensively demonstrated. Psychosomatic research has established that close interrelationships exist between the physical and psychological facets of the total personality. What happens during the actual physical growth process when concomitant severe emotional disturbances

INTRODUCTION

are present, is still a matter of speculation. Most psychiatric clinicians working with children retarded in their physical development have found that the retardation often seems to have its roots in emotional disturbances. Delayed menstruation in girls with severe sexual conflicts is a common example. On the other hand, as will be discussed later, the failure to mature physically at a rate comparable to the other children of the same age group results in real emotional problems for the physically retarded child. These problems, unless wisely handled, may leave severe scars—psychological scars that leave their traces on the individual throughout life.

The shifts in the interaction between physical growth and emotional growth, when both follow the average pattern, can almost be charted. During adolescence, the psychological response of the individual is directly influenced by the particular aspect of physical growth which is in the ascendency. In the early period of rapid physical growth, the characteristic psychological pattern is one of increased ego capacity to deal with reality. When the reproductive organs begin to function, the psychological mechanisms of adjustment are overwhelmed by the impact of the new impulses and the intensification of the older ones. As a result, earlier established ego defenses become inadequate. With the attainment of physical stability at a relatively mature level, the individual again develops capacity for psychological integration. It is usually in this latter period that the individual reveals the underlying nature of his adolescent conflicts, his attempts at solving them, and the goals toward which he is striving.

It should be stressed that adolescence cannot be divided arbitrarily into three sections any more than the entire growth process can be broken down into sharply defined steps of development. The growth process may be compared to a flowing stream upon which a handful of feathers has been cast. Each feather may be likened to a particular aspect of the psychological structure. As the feathers float down the stream certain of them are caught up in a rapidly moving current and advance beyond the others. They may later drift to a stagnant area, while others that had moved at a slower rate overtake the ones in the lead. Some feathers drift to the shore and remain fixed, but ultimately, moving at different tempos, most of them reach the river's outlet—in this analogy, adulthood. As the individual is traveling from birth to maturity, some aspects of his development remain permanently fixed at various points. Some traits will interfere with the development of others; some will carry others forward with them. As with the flowing stream, the natural forces favor the forward movement toward the goal of maturity if other conditions do not interfere. It can be assumed that development in certain areas will be more rapid than in others and that the movement will be influenced by a variety of conditions. Internal and external forces will affect the progress toward maturation in much the same way as the intrinsic and extrinsic factors—the slope of the river's bed and the obstructions impinging from its banks—affect the movement of the feathers journeying down the stream.

I. Physical Aspects of Adolescence

The story of medicine is a fascinating subject to study. The conclusions of the early medical practitioners about phenomena that were not understood often contain a hint of the true significance of the manifestations. Much later, as phenomena were explored, scientific concepts emerged.

A particularly interesting example of such a historical process is seen in the field of psychosomatic medicine. Early prescientific medicine attributed illnesses to the devil's work. The devil, with his talents in witchcraft, now is recognized as a picturesque way of describing symptoms resulting from the interaction of the external environment and multiple internal psychological forces. The goal of psychosomatic medicine might be described as the exploration and clarification of phenomena earlier attributed to witchcraft. Modern concepts give the scientific basis for what was intuitively known in the past—that the physical and the psychological structure and the life experiences of the individual are interacting parts of the total person. The typical manifestations of adolescence provide an excellent demonstration of this interaction.

Adolescence cannot be understood in terms of one discipline, whether that discipline be physical, psychological, sociological, or educational; it is a period of radical change in the total individual. Marked social, psychological, and physical changes are characteristic of this age span and they do not occur unrelated to each other. The physical changes have definite effect on the social and psychological adjustments of the individual; social factors influence the psycho-

9

logical and physical changes; the psychological factors have repercussions both socially and physiologically.

Each aspect of the total person is so interwoven with the others that any attempt to separate them into topics is purely academic. The very fact that, for purposes of clarification, the material in this book is divided into such chapter headings, introduces a falseness to the presentation. It implies that each topic has major significance in itself. Actually, the significance of each isolated phenomenon is relatively unimportant, when the total impact of the interlocking factors is considered. For example, the physical changes that occur in adolescence are important; however, the effect upon the total person of these changes has much greater significance because of their ramified effects—effects that extend far beyond the physical functioning of the body.

As has been pointed out in the introduction, the writer is arbitrarily using the term "adolescence" in this volume to encompass the broad period of change in human development, of which the onset is most clearly demonstrable in the physical changes that occur. This use of the term is broader in scope than the one generally accepted. Dr. Stuart,[1] in an excellent review of studies of growth in adolescence, separates this period into three subdivisions: pre-pubescence, pubescence, and post-pubescence. Others refer to comparable periods as pre-adolescence, adolescence, and post-adolescence. Some authors use the term adolescence to refer only to that period of development following the onset of menstruation in girls and of comparable physiological change in boys. The time immediately preceding is then described as late latency. In the author's opinion, the process is an evolving one, beginning with the spurt in physical growth and continuing until the maturation of the individual is relatively complete. Subdivisions, therefore, seem artificial, giving the impression of steps in development rather than of a fluid process.

Height and Weight

The spurt in growth, heralding the beginning of adolescence, is indicated most clearly in body length (height). The body has been

[1] Harold C. Stuart, M.D., "Physical Growth During Adolescence," *American Journal of Diseases of Children*, LXXIV (1947), 495–502.

growing in length since the time of conception. Growth is rapid in the first two years of life, and then the *rate* of growth decreases, reaching a plateau at about the age of seven in girls and ten in boys. At the age of ten in girls, and a year or two later and less rapidly in boys, the rate of increment increases, reaching its maximum for girls between the ages of twelve and thirteen; in boys this maximum growth occurs one or two years later. Dr. Greulich states: "It will be noted that boys are somewhat taller (longer) than girls at birth and that they maintain this superiority up to about the age of ten years, at which time the girls equal the boys in stature. From the ages of eleven to fourteen years the girls are taller than the boys, but by the age of fifteen years the boys have grown slightly taller than the girls. The boys' superiority in stature increases during the next four years and is maintained thereafter." [2]

Studies of growth indicate that some variation exists in different social or ethnic groups studied. The variation, however, is chiefly a difference in the age of onset of the growth spurt, rather than a difference in the general pattern. A spurt occurs coincident with the time at which the secondary sex characteristics begin to develop and the primary sex organs begin to function. This introduces another significant consideration which is of particular importance when the individual, rather than the statistically average, growth period is considered. Each physically healthy individual will show a growth pattern that, charted, will resemble the average curve.

The curve for the individual, however, cannot be superimposed on the average curve if the chronological age is used as the basis for comparison. On the other hand, if instead of the chronological age the physiological age (which can be established for girls by utilizing the years just preceding and just following the onset of menstruation) is used, the curves of growth will be relatively similar. Where the spurt of growth occurs early, however, the ultimate increment in height will tend to be less. When the spurt occurs chronologically late the increase in height will tend to be greater.

A combined study of groups by which the statistical average of growth is determined and a study of individual growth patterns suggest that there is a normal growth process during which character-

[2] William W. Greulich, "Some Observations on the Growth and Development of Adolescent Children," *Journal of Pediatrics*, XIX (1941), 305.

istic changes occur. The time of onset and the magnitude of these changes vary widely from individual to individual. The developmental age of an individual must be judged at any given time according to his own pattern of growth instead of according to the "average pattern." The onset of physical adolescence and its completion will vary in individuals. Within that period, however, characteristic modifications will occur which coincide with the "statistically average pattern." Physical adolescence will be understood more clearly if it is considered a period of accelerated maturation rather than a chronological age span.

The weight of an individual also increases more rapidly during adolescence than during the preceding period. The increase increment in weight is less marked than that observed in height and extends over a longer period of time. The increase in height during early adolescence and other changes in the skeletal structure—changes that result in broadening of the total skeleton, and increased massiveness of individual bones—account in part for the increase in weight. This is particularly true during the period immediately followng the spurt in growth. Muscles are also growing rapidly. This is particularly true immediately following the leveling off of the rate of height increment. The fact that the muscle growth continues after the skeletal structure has reached its maximum partially explains why weight increase continues after cessation of increase in body length.

Sex Characteristics

The development of primary and secondary sex characteristics follows a typical pattern. Again one observes a variation in the age of onset of these changes between boys and girls and between individuals of the same sex. Such changes usually occur in girls approximately two years earlier than in boys. In the female, during normal puberty, the development of the breasts is one of the earliest manifestations of beginning sexual maturation. These breast changes begin before pubic hair appears. Axillary hair develops later than pubic hair and usually does not appear until the first menstruation.

In the male the pubic hair is the first secondary sex characteristic to appear, coming shortly after the primary sex organs show signs of increase in size. Later, axillary hair develops and then facial hair

PHYSICAL ASPECTS OF ADOLESCENCE

appears. At about the time axillary hair appears, an enlargement of the breast tissue frequently occurs; it disappears after a variable number of months. The voice change, which is so often used as a criterion for the onset of puberty, actually occurs late in the adolescent period. The voice change is an indication that typical adolescent bodily changes are fairly well advanced.

The development of the primary sex organs is of great significance in the physical development of adolescence. It is often falsely assumed that the onset of menstruation is indicative of physical maturation in the girl. Typically, at the time of the onset of menstruation the ovaries have reached about 30 per cent of adult size. The full development of both the testes and ovaries occurs after the period of maximum growth in length is completed, and thus at a considerably later time than can be assumed from such external manifestations as menstruation. A hormone is produced by the anterior lobe of the pituitary gland, which governs the growth and functioning of the ovaries and testes. When the pituitary gland secretes this hormone in quantities sufficient to stimulate growth in the immature sex glands, a sex hormone begins to be produced by the ovaries in the female and by the testes in the male. The female hormone stimulates the growth of the secondary sex characteristics as well as the growth of the primary sex organs. The male hormone similarly stimulates the development of the male secondary sex characteristics and the primary sex organs.

Menstruation indicates that the girl has begun her progress toward sexual maturity, with the quantity of hormones produced being sufficient to bring about changes in the uterus which result in the onset of menstruation. There is considerable evidence that the girl at this period is probably sterile. Physical sexual development continues and finally reaches the point at which the ovary produces a fertilizable ovum. During the early period of maturation of the sex glands, irregular menstruation is frequently found and is not indicative of any abnormality but rather of the relative immaturity of the sex organs.

This delay in fertility observed in girls has its counterpart in the sexual development of boys. Mature spermatozoa usually are not present in any appreciable quantity until the age of fifteen or sixteen, although there is some evidence of a relative increase in sperm formation beginning at about the age of thirteen. The mature functioning of the testes, as indicated by the production of live sperm, occurs at the end of the period of rapid physical growth and when the secondary sexual characteristics are well advanced.

It is impossible, within the limits of this book, to describe in detail the interaction of the glands of internal secretion. There are still many unknown factors involved which are the subject of continued research by endocrinologists. On the basis of present knowledge, certain generalizations may be formulated. The glands of internal secretion have a mutually interacting function. They also affect the general functioning of the body. They have an equal interrelationship with the psychological structure of the individual. During adolescence the multiple interacting forces are in the process of change, progressing toward a point of physical maturity. Only when physical maturity is reached is a relative stabilization of the interacting physical forces attained.

Physical Co-ordination

In view of the common concept that adolescents are awkward, the results of tests of physical strength, of endurance, and of motor co-ordination are surprising. Studies have been reported indicating that physical strength, motor ability, and motor co-ordination increase during adolescence. Charts reproduced in *The Adolescent Period: A Graphic Atlas* [3] indicate that the boy from the age of thirteen to seventeen shows a rapid increase in strength. While the girl's strength increases, it does not increase as rapidly as does the boy's. Another chart showing motor co-ordination, cited in the same monograph, reveals that the development of motor skills increases up to the age of fourteen in one test and continues beyond that period in another. Further tests have indicated that motor co-ordination in boys steadily increases until about the age of seventeen. In girls it improves until about the age of fourteen, followed by some decline at that time. These tests suggest that the awkwardness of adolescence has significance other than that of a breakdown in the ability to co-ordinate during this period.

[3] Frank K. Shuttleworth, *The Adolescent Period: A Graphic Atlas*, Monograph of the Society for Research in Child Development, Inc., Vol. XIV, Serial No. 49, No. 1, 1949. Child Development Publications of the Society for Research in Child Development, Northwestern University, Evanston, Illinois.

Climate and Nutrition

Although, in general, the rate of maturation is probably an inherent characteristic of the particular individual, it is affected by the environment. There is evidence that climate has some bearing on the rate of maturation. More significantly, from the individual standpoint, nutrition affects the rate of maturation. During periods of rapid growth, the body needs are greater than they are during periods of slow growth.[4] The adolescent requirements in terms of minerals and calories are greater than they are at an earlier period. During periods of rapid growth the organism probably has less reserve with which to deal with extra strain. The demands of a particular environment or a particular activity may therefore prove an excessive strain on one individual whereas another individual may be able to handle such demands quite adequately.

[4] Harry A. Waisman, M.D., Julius B. Richmond, and Starks J. Williams, "Vitamin Requirements in Adolescence," *Journal of Pediatrics*, XXXVII (1950), 922–935.

II. Psychological Growth Patterns

impulse toward Growth

INHERENT IN THE STRUCTURE of the young living organism is an impulse toward growth. This is self-evident so far as the physical development of the organism is concerned; probably it is equally true of the psychological structure. The growth impulse both physically and psychologically is toward maturation. As indicated in the preceding chapter, while the individual has been growing since conception, the rate varies at different ages. A period of accelerated physical growth begins at about the age of ten in girls and of twelve in boys. No yardsticks are available to measure accurately the rate of emotional growth of the individual comparable to those available for measuring physical growth. Clinically, however, there is evidence that while emotional growth is a continuing process up to adulthood, there are periods in which the rate of growth is slow, and others in which it is more rapid.

The so-called latency phase of psychological development is one of relatively slow but very significant change. During the latency period the child is gradually mastering his reality. This is possible because he has discovered ways of dealing with his primitive impulses and his infantile conflicts which are compatible, relatively, with the demands of the reality world and of his own conscience. Thus, latency is characterized by increasing ego strength except in those cases in which the child is struggling with conflicts of such intensity that his ego is powerless to deal with them. The average child during latency gives the impression of being increasingly comfortable in his environment.

PSYCHOLOGICAL GROWTH PATTERNS

Ego Development in Early Adolescence

There is clinical evidence that, at about the time when the pediatrician observes a more rapid rate in physical growth, a similar acceleration in ego development takes place, manifested by an intensification of the urge toward maturation with an accompanying increased capacity for adaptation. Conscious anxiety in the average child at this time is at a minimum. He approaches his social group with confidence. He participates in games that involve skill and team co-operation. He plays and studies, he argues with parents and friends, he enjoys pleasant experiences and protests against unpleasant ones, with a minimum of manifest anxiety and guilt. He assumes responsibilities within the framework of his reality. His evaluation of reality may differ greatly from that of his parents. To him it may be important to finish a game; to his parents it may be more important that he go to bed. It may be more important to him to make a model airplane than to shovel snow from a sidewalk, a conviction that the parents do not share. The difficulty between the child and the parents may then be a difference in values; it is not necessarily indicative of deep conflicts in the child-parent relationship.

The child at this age objects to those aspects of reality he does not like and he attempts to circumvent these undesirable aspects if he can. If he cannot circumvent them he makes what is to him a realistic adjustment to them. He is less apt than a younger child to succumb to a neurotic solution of the problems he faces. It is not that a child never utilizes neurotic defenses at this age; it is rather that, relatively, considering the intensity of the internal conflicts and the frustrating reality, the child's ego has greater adaptive power. If the pressure is too great, the ego, in spite of optimum functioning, may prove inadequate to the task at hand and neurotic defenses may develop.

Because of the strength of the ego during this period, episodes that inevitably have deep emotional significance frequently are handled with surprising facility, at least for the time being. This is well illustrated in the adjustment made to the loss of a parent or a sibling during this age period. At the time the tragedy is experienced the child appears to meet the trauma realistically by accepting it and by readily turning to other activities and interests. That the trauma had an effect is apparent later if the individual who experienced it undergoes psychoanalytical therapy. It then becomes clear that the emotional implications of the experience were muted, repressed, or denied, and that the ego mastered the anxiety aroused by a threatened disintegration of the child's world by flight into reality. The experience was dealt with as a part of external reality, with a repression of its emotionally charged meaning. When the traumatic event occurred the ego adjustment was of such nature that the underlying conflicts were completely hidden not only from the observer but also from the individual himself.

In many American communities at present a discernible cultural pattern exists in this age group which probably illustrates the increased desire for maturation. It is true that, as a result of a more casual relationship between boys and girls all through childhood, a much greater acceptance of each other at all ages is now observed than was manifested in the past when the two sexes were kept more apart and when different patterns of interest and behavior were imposed on each sex. The interest of each sex in the other shows a marked acceleration in the latter half of the grammar school period. Girls and boys begin dating, have mixed parties, and verbalize an interest in each other, not only because of shared activities but because of sexual differences. At first glance this seems to imply an early sexual maturation. If these children are observed carefully, however, it can be seen that they are playing a game. Most of them are playing at being sexually interested in each other, whereas actually they are not yet ready emotionally for a genuine interest of this nature. This behavior is to them evidence of growing up. It has value to them not because it is meeting an internal sexual need, but because it implies leaving childhood behind and taking on the patterns of an older age group. It is true that in a certain number of cases children do act out a sexual conflict that has its roots in unresolved infantile conflicts that were not sufficiently redirected or repressed; but these children are disturbed children. A large percentage of this age group in our culture, however, are not disturbed, but are playing a part which to them represents being grown up.

The wish to be more grown up creates a problem for the child. He realizes, perhaps consciouly, that he is only playing a part. The realization results in a sense of inadequacy since he really is not what he wishes he were; he tries hard to fulfil a role for which he is not prepared. The result is a caricature of adulthood. Such pseudo-maturity is even more striking when seen in contrast to his total behavior, which is still characteristically that of living in the day-by-day, child reality of school, of play, of friends, and of home.

Body Strangeness

In this period of rapid growth the child's body becomes unfamiliar to him. As one boy said, "I don't think that I'm really awkward, it's just that my feet are so far away from my head these days." One girl whose growth had been extremely rapid expressed what, at first glance, seemed to indicate a sense of depersonalization. The significance of the reaction, however, was minimal when viewed in the light of her total personality structure; she described a feeling that the ground was so far away from her when she walked that she was afraid she might not reach it.

In addition to the actual change in stature, secondary sex characteristics begin to appear. The growth of pubic hair, the modification of childish contours, the development of the breasts, and the change in the external genitalia all add to the feeling of body unfamiliarity.

The unfamiliarity with the body may explain the apparent discrepancy between the actual clinical tests of motor co-ordination and the casual observation of the child in his day-by-day living. It was noted in the previous chapter that tests indicate that during the period of rapid physical growth there is also an increase in manual dexterity and muscle control. Since the young adolescent is usually described as awkward, these findings seem contrary to common observation. The contradiction may not be as great as it appears. It is possible that, when movements are limited to a defined goal within a limited framework, the individual is able to function well. When movements are not purposefully determined within the narrow limits of such a defined situation but have to do rather with general adaptation to sudden stimuli or sudden impulses, awkwardness appears. In the latter instance the individual attempts to handle a body whose structure is unfamiliar because of its recent changes, without the assistance of a learned pattern. As a result the awkward adolescent boy may be an extremely graceful swimmer because he has learned to swim. When he does not know what to do with his feet he is awkward with them. This may also explain why the awkward adolescent girl responds so quickly to training in walking and postural control. The metamorphosis that a modeling school can effect in the awkward adolescent girl represents the potential co-ordinating ability of the individual, an ability not previously utilized because of unfamiliarity with the new body. Whenever a pattern for using the body is established through a learned technique, the ability to co-ordinate becomes evident.

Adaptive Expectations

On the whole, in spite of the problem of adjusting to the newly shaping body, and in spite of the pressure toward maturation, this period is typically a relatively comfortable time both for the child and the adults responsible for him. Parents feel reassured when the child—who they were not sure was ever going to establish himself as an independent individual—becomes reasonable, reliable, and capable of handling responsibility. That educators recognize the change is indicated in the educational program. The curriculum for this age group is enriched by social and scientific studies, and by emphasis on discussion groups in literature, art, and political science. Society assumes that a child of this age has accepted certain mores. Stealing now is seen as delinquent behavior whereas at an earlier age it was looked upon as an understandable manifestation of immaturity. The child is expected to get to school on time and to come home at a reasonable hour. His failure to do so is met by irritation on the part of the adult, implying that the child is "old enough to know better." The attitudes of the home, the school, and other social groups denote that the child is expected to have made a successful adjustment to the demands of reality.

Breakdown of Adaptation

The peaceful state described above is of short duration. The transition from this early period of adolescence to the next phase is anything but a smooth one. It is easier to correlate this change with the growth pattern of girls than of boys because of the sharp temporal delineation that menstruation offers. From six months to a year before the onset of menstruation a girl may become increasingly irritable. At home she may seem fatigued and often depressed. Among her friends she may be sensitive, easily hurt, and perhaps quarrelsome. Her teachers may observe her sensitivity and irritability. They may notice that she is not so reliable or conscientious as in the past. Concurrently she may make increased demands for greater independence, for privileges like those of the older age group, and for permission to emulate behavior she associates with adult living. She wants to wear lipstick and high heels and to have long formal dresses. She wants to stay out later. She wants to date whom she pleases and to do what she pleases. But she cries because she cannot have a piece of candy!

Hypochondriasis

During this early period of adolescence and continuing until maturity is attained, the child may complain of many physical symptoms. He may show a great deal of concern as to what these symptoms may mean. He has become a "hypochondriac." Before it is assumed that these complaints are invalid, a careful medical study should be made to rule out actual physical pathology. It is important to bear in mind that during periods of rapid physical growth a child has greater need for certain specific foods. The diets of adolescents may well be inadequate in view of the rapid growth that is occurring. As a result, some of the physical symptoms about which the adolescent complains may actually represent a relative, sub-clinical malnutrition. These complaints are often ill-defined. No one except a physician, and then only after he has made a careful study of the physical condition of his patient, should assume that these complaints are psychological rather than physical.

Frequently, true hypochondriacal symptoms do develop during adolescence. There are several possible explanations and the basic cause will differ with various individuals. In certain instances the physical discomforts are actually experienced but are identical with sensations that have always been present. The individual reacts to them with greater sensitivity and awareness than previously. The reaction appears to be similar to one characteristic of infancy. The neuro-sensory system is, in infancy, especially reactive to physical sensation. During early childhood, individuals become familiar with and therefore ignore many physical sensations to which they responded earlier.

A simple example will demonstrate this acclimation to physical discomfort. An infant who is too warm will wake up fussy and restless, suggesting that the physical discomfort has interfered with his sleep. As he grows older, much greater discomfort from overwarmth is required before his sleep will be interfered with. He has acquired a mechanism for ignoring mild physical discomfort. During adolescence the sensitive awareness of body sensation returns. Many "hypochondriacal" symptoms observed in adolescents may be responses to previously ignored stimuli.

In other instances, the unfamiliarity with the body as discussed earlier undoubtedly plays a part in the complaint of physical symptoms. The "hypochondriasis" then is an indication of the anxiety aroused by the physical changes occurring. One situation in which this is apparent is in response to the temporary breast development in boys during the early adolescent period. Boys often show considerable concern about this manifestation, feeling that it indicates effeminacy. Similarly, not infrequently girls complain about abdominal pain a few months before the onset of menstruation. The exact basis for this pain is not too clear. Girls themselves often associate it with the approaching first menstrual period and express considerable concern about the coming event. While a frank discussion of menstruation often relieves a certain part of the conscious anxiety regarding it, the basic anxiety is not relieved in a large percentage of girls. The period ahead is that of the great unknown. The anxiety that this anticipation creates expresses itself then in physical symptoms.

Acne at adolescence presents a specific problem. The reasons adolescents develop acne are again multiple; the physical changes that are occurring and the resultant glandular imbalance are factors. The adolescent's poor food habits often cause an exacerbation of the acne. Emotional problems certainly accentuate the difficulty in many instances. The acne in itself is disturbing and a vicious circle, psychologically, is established. The adolescent often associates the acne with being "dirty," a feeling based upon reality as indicated by the doctor's insistence upon cleanliness. The adolescent may feel, however, that the importance of dirt relates not only to external "dirt" but also to his own internal, concealed "dirtiness." In the past the adolescent frequently associated acne with frequent masturbation; the association is probably less frequent now because of the more tolerant attitude taken toward masturbation. Acne still, in many instances, means to the child that his otherwise secret sin, of whatever nature, is being shown to the world.

The mechanism of displacement may also account for many physical complaints. The anxiety about physical sensation becomes a symbolic representation of the basic anxiety concerning adjustment. The adolescent feels uneasy and attempts to structuralize the uneasiness by relating it to his physical well-being. Physical concerns are easier to face, easier to expose to others, and easier to find reassurance for than are the ill-defined, nebulous, psychological sources of anxiety.

Effect of Reproductive Glands

Revolutionary changes are taking place in the body, particularly in the glands of internal secretion. Before the onset of menstruation, and the corresponding developmental changes in boys, the sexual glands are beginning to function. The effectiveness of the secretion of these glands has a bearing not only on the physical development and physical functioning of the body, but also has a direct effect on the psychological response of the individual. There are waves of new feelings accompanied by intensification of old ones. Clinical observations suggest that these changes occur not in mild ripples of gradually increasing volume, but actually with the intensity of breakers that flow over the individual and overwhelm him. The average adolescent lives through a period, sometimes of fairly short duration, in which he seems to have lost a good part of his capacity to deal with reality; his emotional state borders on panic. In the relatively normal child this period is not too striking. He appears somewhat anxious; he may relate dreams of nightmarish quality in which his panic and disorganization are more discernible than in his waking hours. In school he may seem to study but not be able to learn; he may have difficulty in concentrating and may be extremely restless in his activities. He may appear to be basically confused, a confusion partially disguised by a veneer of ego adaptation. Such a period is much more likely to occur in the child whose developmental history has indicated continual emotional disturbance. If his contact with reality has always been tenuous, at this period an even more precarious relationship with reality is frequently observed. The child suffering from so-called infantile psychosis often shows a marked exacerbation of the mental symptoms. In contrast to the really ill child, the normal child presents only minor symptoms. Close observation of adolescent groups suggests, however, that practically every child is somewhat overwhelmed for a short period by the effects of the physiological maturing process. His defenses are inadequate to deal with the strain to which he is exposed.

Mobilization of Defenses

Gradually the individual mobilizes his defenses. Probably the process of reorganizing the defenses begins in the individual after the glands of internal secretion have established a new interacting balance. The reproductive glands will continue to grow for some time, with a resultant increase in hormonal secretion. This change, however, is one of increase rather than change in function; relative physical stabilization has been attained. The individual then has an opportunity to re-establish defenses against forces that are no longer shifting as they were during the immediately preceding period. Psychological integration is difficult to attain until physiological integration has been partially established. During the period of physiological prestabilization, any attempt to build a psychological structure is to build on shifting sands. Once relative physiological stability occurs, the psychological structure can be built on a firmer foundation.

Re-establishment of the defenses is not an easy achievement. As will be discussed in the following chapters, old defenses prove inadequate and new ones must be established. An appreciable period—months or perhaps years—is needed for the individual to find solutions to underlying problems that developed earlier and have now increased in intensity, or to problems that have been newly acquired. From a psychological standpoint, this period is the one referred to in any discussion of the emotional problems of adolescence.

It is important to stress that the onset of activity of the reproductive glands not only results in a heightening of the sexual responsiveness of the individual and an increased somatic sensitiveness but also in a general increase in sensitivity. During the entire period of adolescence, the individual is more responsive to all stimuli. The sunset, which in pre-adolescence was meaningful only as a signal to return home for dinner, now at adolescence becomes an esthetic experience. It becomes beautiful, depressing, or stimulating. Trees, which previously were of value only for climbing, now take on symbolic meanings. Music, which was a matter of rhythm or melody, is now associated with all the emotional turmoil of the individual. Thoughts that were previously accepted or discarded on the basis of their reality functioning now take on poetic coloring. The individual may be compared to a violin. Previously the instrument may have seemed to be a cigar box strung with catgut; at adolescence it may seem suddenly to have become a Stradivarius. Played on by varying forces, it sometimes responds as if played by a concertmaster, at other times as if by an untalented amateur. At times it refuses to produce music at all.

III. Social Pressures

IN ANY STUDY OF THE PROBLEMS of the adolescent it is important to give proper weight to the social pressures to which he is exposed. In our culture, society not only makes heavy demands upon the adolescent, but it fails to provide him with a preconceived and carefully outlined pattern to help him meet these demands. This is in contrast to many of the primitive cultures. The initiation ceremonies in primitive cultures establish an arbitrary line between childhood and adulthood. Prohibitions and sanctions govern, define, and free the behavior of childhood. At a certain point, with ritualistic ceremony, the individual is made an adult. From that time on he is expected to live in the adult world according to a defined code. Taboos and customs give him a framework in which to develop his own personality. These taboos and codes are not controversial. It is not for the young adult to decide whether or not he will obey them; failure to do so results in arbitrary punishment while compliance results in acceptance. The immutability of the standard not only is unquestioned by the older adults but is also accepted by his own age group. He can be secure if he obeys. He is secure not only in his relationship with his social world—his superiors, his peers, and his inferiors—but he is also secure in his own conviction of being an adult. This security rests on his observance of the taboos placed upon him and on his acceptance of the privileges granted to adults.

Quite an opposite milieu for the adolescent exists in our culture, particularly in a country that places value on democracy and the

SOCIAL PRESSURES

rights of the individual. In a democracy it is believed, at least in theory, that one has the inalienable right to develop as an individual so long as other individuals are not jeopardized. The concepts of individual growth and of conformity to a pattern are incompatible. It is believed, moreover, that both adulthood and culture are enriched if the individual is allowed to grow into adulthood rather than being molded into it. The lack of an equivalent of an initiation ceremony increases the confusion and anxiety of the adolescent. His behavior is unpredictable because it is determined by the confusion within him; he is not protected by enforced compliance to well-established rituals and laws. He is told in effect to grow up—to achieve an undefined state. He is not told *how* to grow up.

Emphasis on Self-Development

Although in principle our culture places value on the individual's right to choose his own pattern of self-development, in practice it penalizes those who do not recognize the difference between license and liberty. Certain controls of the behavior of individuals are essential for the maintenance of society. Such standards, however, are difficult to formulate and do not have the rigidity of the taboos of a primitive society. Because of the difficulty in formulating standards, and the complexity of translating them into the realities of social living, together with the difficulty of integrating them within the framework of individual rights, the concept of acceptable behavior is a confused one. The adolescent, unsure of his own goals, keenly feels the impact of the social confusion. Because of his own confusion, he seeks an answer outside himself. He tries to find it both in his own family group and in the world outside his family. Neither group can give him rules of living which are without contradiction. He is sharply aware of the confusions in our social structure.

It is not necessary to go into the broader areas of ethics, politics, business, or international relations to document these confusions. The most significant confusion the child experiences is in his own home; for example, in the attitude of the typical parent toward dating. The boy who is not dating girls is a source of concern to his parents. They feel that perhaps he is not maturing correctly;

27

something is retarding his normal maturation. They press him to date girls, tease him about his self-consciousness, and imply that he should be more tolerant of his natural impulses. Finally he does date girls. The parents then become concerned because he is staying out late, he is not studying as much as he should, and they feel that he may not have sufficient understanding of the risks involved in his relationships with girls. They then warn him of the dangers inherent in his own natural impulses.

His parents keep reminding him that he is growing up. They say he should be able to assume more responsibility. He should think more for himself and be less dependent upon them for guidance. When he attempts, on the other hand, to be more independent they remind him that after all they are still his parents and he is too young to know what is best for him. They have a right to control him until he is of age. Often, what they actually mean by independence is that he should take more initiative in doing what they wish him to do. But what they wish is rarely very clear. They expect him to be "grown up" in the sense of possessing all the virtues parents value, and yet to lack all the vices usually tolerated by adults in one another. Few parents ever reach peace within themselves to the extent that they actually approve of the adolescent's doing what they have told him to do.

A word in defense of parents' conflicting attitudes should be offered. Parents of an adolescent are often frightened people. They see their child as an extension of themselves, growing, they hope, into a more nearly adequate adult than either of them is. Their wish derives not only from pride in their own child but also from an honest desire that their child should have a happier adult life than they themselves have had. They sense the confusion of the adolescent and are frightened by it. They also sense the impact of biological urges. They recognize that the adolescent as yet does not have the tools with which to deal constructively with these internal impulses. They look back upon their own adolescence and recall it as a time of stress in which they were apparently in grave danger of ruining their lives. By some miracle they were saved from destroying their potentialities, a destruction that seems, in retrospect, to have been imminent. They fear that the same fortuitous circumstances that saved them may not be present to save their child. They do not wish to trust to the fate

SOCIAL PRESSURES

by which their past was protected as the instrument for safeguarding their own child. They want their child to develop into a heterosexual adult, yet they are fearful that he cannot avoid the pitfalls of that development. They wish him to be independent but they are fearful that he cannot handle independence without their guidance. Most parents, consciously at least, wish their child to grow up to be a happy adult. They are frightened by their own roles in this process.

It is equally true that many parents, while they consciously wish their child to grow up, actually are resistant to this process. Perhaps they cannot face the vacuum that will exist when the child is no longer dependent upon them. Sometimes they are jealous of the child entering early adulthood with all its apparent glamor when their own adulthood seems tarnished. Many of them express their own neuroses in handling their adolescent son or daughter. The father may unconsciously fear to compete with his mature son because his son may experience greater success than he and thus point up the father's inadequacy. In other instances the father may fear that his boy will be as inadequate as he himself is. The son's failure will be his own failure and thus he tries to delay the evil day when he will be doubly exposed. The father may be so emotionally tied to his daughter that he cannot give her up to another man. He may strive to keep her a child to avoid the implications of his love for her if she becomes a mature woman. Whatever may be the hidden conflict in the relationship with the child, the unconscious motivation of parental behavior toward the child is often in contrast to the conscious motivation. Regardless of what produced the conflict, parents as well as adolescents are confused, and the confusion of each adds to the confusion of the other.

Conflicting Standards

The confusion of the adolescent is increased by the half-truths he learned during childhood, half-truths that were told him in good faith. Usually they represent the ideals to which adults wish to cling; the truth, which they evade, often represents the compromises they have made with those ideals. The concept of democracy is an illustration of this point. The child is told that people should be valued for what they are instead of what they have. He is taught to value persons, regardless of their race, creed, or economic status. This point of view is considered practical while he mingles on the playgrounds and forms childhood friendships. However, when he approaches the time for choosing his permanent social group and his permanent life mate, he is confronted with a different set of values. He is then told that it is wiser to select one's social group and to choose one's mate from persons with backgrounds and beliefs similar to one's own. In one community in which there were approximately the same number of Jewish and Gentile families, considerable pride was expressed by the parents in the community because the Jewish and Gentile children intermingled with no evidence of awareness that some of the children were Jewish and some Gentile. As the particular group entered high school, the parents manifested increasing concern. Jewish boys dated Gentile girls; Gentile boys dated Jewish girls. Many adolescents discovered that while their parents accepted intermarriage between Jews and Gentiles in theory, they did not want their own children exposed to the problems of intermarriage. The young people, therefore, were exposed to a contradiction between what they had been taught and what the parents really expected of them.

Acceptance of the value of sex education for children has resulted in the adolescent's reaching his physiological sexual maturity knowing only half the truth. Since skills have not yet been developed for telling the whole truth, sex information has carried an implication that sex is desirable, acceptable, and something to be recognized without guilt as a part of living. It is mentioned, of course, that sex is something that finds its most complete expression in marriage. To the small child such a statement seems a parenthetical remark, and probably has little significance to him. With the maturation of his sexual drive he faces what may appear to him an attitude incompatible with that implied when, in childhood, he was first told about sex. He is told that he should not gratify his sexual impulses; sexual freedom is now frowned upon. He must wait. He is likely to see the new point of view as a contradiction of the earlier parental attitude rather than to recognize that now he is learning the whole truth whereas before he learned only half of it.

School and Free Time Activities

The educational system adds an additional burden to the adolescent. As will be discussed in a later chapter, the adolescent has a great need for someone to whom to turn on a dependency level. During his period in school up to the junior high school level, he has had his teacher as a parent-substitute to guide him in his learning process. Because of the continuity through the day of this relationship, his teacher has had meaning to him as an individual. The junior and senior high schools deprive him of this relationship. The school experience now is geared primarily to subject matter and the teacher becomes a mere instrument for teaching the subject. His contact with the teacher is limited in most instances to his class work and the subject matter of his course. The school system attempts to meet this problem by providing advisers, deans, and vocational counselors. Usually such specialists are not an integral part of the everyday school life of the child; he views them as persons set apart, filling a special role. The adolescent's school experience is actually in terms of subject matter rather than of personal relationships with the faculty, at a time when an impersonal relationship is gratifying to him because it allows him to retreat, but also can be frustrating if he wishes help. He may find a member of the faculty who will serve as a guiding, supporting person to him, but this usually occurs as a result of his own seeking or through the initiative of a particular teacher, not because it is inherent in the educational program as it was earlier.

Such an impersonal setting is obviously more characteristic of large schools than of smaller ones. With the growing tendency to increase the size of the high schools in order to broaden the curriculum, the educational system is depriving the adolescent of the support he might obtain were he in a smaller educational framework. The advantage of subject teaching is partially negated unless the high school faculty has not only an understanding of the adolescent but also an alert interest in the total personality of the individual. In the author's experience, many high school teachers interpret the adolescent's indifference to a subject as a personal attack upon the teacher. As a result, the teacher reacts with hostility toward the student and widens the gulf between the teacher and the child at a time when the latter may badly need support.

The stimulation the adolescent receives in his free time adds further to his confusion. The movies have been so condemned that one hesitates even to mention the possible implications they may have for the adolescent. It should be noted, however, that movies, radio and television programs, novels, and plays to which the adolescent is exposed are actually a source of education to him, not only about practical world events, but also about the way people live and feel. If reality is the criterion, most of the portrayals of life shown by these media represent only caricatures; still, the superficial falseness is more apparent than real. Frequently the portrayals are representative of raw human emotions and human fantasy, stripped of many of the social defenses that are a part of the normal adjustment to living. As such, they appeal to the basic human strivings of people.

The presentation appears as a caricature because it is not in focus. While purporting to be a true portrayal of emotional experiences, actually the picture is fragmented and thus incomplete. Because the fragments are valid but are divorced from other parts of the total psychological structure, they expose the observer to pressure for emotional release of repressed feelings. This pressure is neutralized in reality living by counter-pressures. The counter-pressures are less powerful or perhaps absent in the dramatic performance. Thus, again, the entertainment world, as so many other experiences, offers not the truth but only a half-truth.

To the adolescent these portrayals may be both frightening and overstimulating. He may be afraid of the feelings that are aroused because of his unconscious fear that his controls will break down. On the other hand, the dramas may strengthen the repressed emotional drives so that the adolescent is forced to face some of the emotions that actually need to be freed from too severe repression if he is to mature to healthy psychological adulthood. Thus, the effect of the stimulation is not entirely unfortunate so far as the ultimate development of the adolescent is concerned. It may, however, contribute to confusion in the adolescent period.

With even limited imagination one can easily expand the confusing picture the adolescent faces in his reality world. Again

SOCIAL PRESSURES

it should be stressed that the confusion is not necessarily unfortunate in the light of the goals our culture has set for the development of human personality. Both the individual and our culture would benefit if it were possible to determine the maximum amount of confusion that an individual can tolerate at any given time. If his experiences could be limited to tolerable confusion until he has mastered one of its aspects, to be followed steplike by another exposure and subsequent mastery, many of the disasters during and following adolescence might be avoided. As a result, he might reach adulthood better equipped to solve the problems imposed by society—to find solutions that might give the individual a satisfactory adulthood and increase his capacity to participate as an adult in a constructive manner in his social world. To dream of such a situation, certainly at the present time, is to dream of Utopia. At present, the adolescent confusion is unavoidable. Since the degree of confusion may be too great for the individual adolescent to handle wisely, it is important that those interested in him recognize the pressures to which he is exposed. If this is done, it may be possible to lessen the traumatic impact of this period by alleviating the pressures or, if the pressures are unavoidable, by supporting him through this period.

Variations in Development

Social pressures have particular repercussions for certain adolescents. As has been indicated, adolescence is not wholly a chronological period, but represents a physiological and psychological span. Because of the variation in rate of maturation in different individuals, it is impossible to establish any arbitrary chronological age as representing the onset of a particular individual's adolescence. For example, while it is statistically true that the average girl manifests the maximum spurt physically at the age of twelve, the onset of such growth may deviate from the average by as much as two or three years. This is equally true of psychological maturation. Two persons of identical chronological age may be at very different stages of psychological maturation. One may be struggling with the full impact of psychological adolescence, while the other may still be handling his life situation with the responses characteristic of the latency period. Our society, in spite of its theoretical respect for individuality, tends to judge individuals by the criteria of statistical norms. As a result, the child who matures early may be considered maladjusted only because he presents the phenomena of adolescent behavior when, according to norms for his chronological age, he should be behaving quite differently. Similarly, the child who matures late is placed in an environment that is geared to a more psychologically mature pattern of behavior. Again, he may be considered a maladjusted child if he does not meet the criteria used to judge "normal" development. Actually, his behavior may be quite "normal" if the level of his emotional maturation is properly placed.

Variations in growth patterns create problems for the individual not only because of the standardization of our cultural program, but also because of his relationship to his own chronological age group. The child whose rate of growth is markedly different from that of the norm may find himself alienated from his chronological peers. The child whose maturation occurs early is aware that he is becoming different from his friends. He has difficulty in finding common ground with them because his feelings, his tensions, and his needs are quite alien to the group. Not only does he sense that adults frown upon him, but he finds no support in children of his own age. He feels drawn to those who actually are, from the standpoint of maturation, more truly his contemporaries. Because these individuals, however, are chronologically older, they are not too accessible to him. They may also fail to accept him because young people as well as adults consider chronological age the real indication of the individual's level of maturation. Furthermore, while the individuals in this older age group from many standpoints may be his true contemporaries, they have had a longer period of realistic experiences and therefore are actually more advanced. For example, a boy of thirteen, if his rate of maturation has been rapid, may, psychologically, be a contemporary of a boy of fifteen. On the football field, however, the 15-year-old boy has had a longer time to develop skills in the game and the 13-year-old boy may not be able to play an equally good game. He would therefore be rejected by the 15-year-old boy in spite of the common ground of psychological maturity. As a result, the individual who matures early often finds himself isolated because he is out of step with his chronological age group and excluded from

SOCIAL PRESSURES

an older age group. He may attempt to fill the social vacuum he experiences by a richer internal living, and by developing secondary defenses that may have an unfortunate effect on his later personality development. It is often extremely difficult to determine how much of his manifest behavior is the direct result of his early maturation and how much is a defense against the problems created by his deviation.

The opposite social problem arises when the child's development is slower than the average rate. Then, instead of the environment's failing to meet the needs for enriched experiences, it exposes the child to demands that he is not yet ready to meet. His peer group, too, is emotionally alien to him; he does not feel as they do. In no area is this more manifest than in the developing interest in the opposite sex. Often a girl of thirteen will see her friends interested in boys, enjoying dating, and in the throes of the confusion resulting from the physiological sexual maturation that is occurring. The girl who has not reached this stage of physical development has no genuine empathy with the girls who have. She may seek to solve this by finding companionship in a younger age group. She may be subject then to this group's rebuffs, since the younger age group does not consider her a true peer. Furthermore, her attempt to find satisfaction in social relationships with younger children, who represent her psychological peers, will be frowned upon by adults and will be met with contempt from her chronological peers with whom in the past she has found her social acceptance. This may mean to her that she is abnormal—that she is queer. The resultant anxiety may be quite overpowering. She may succumb to her own sense of inadequacy and accept the rebuff and implied opinion of her old group that she is an inferior person. She may attempt to deny her inadequacy and by imitation play a role that requires greater maturity than she really has. Often this acting-out behavior not only alienates her peer group but also brings upon her severe criticism and rejection by adults. As in the child who developed too rapidly, a secondary character disorder may develop, not because the individual has deeply rooted conflicts that cannot be resolved but because her slow rate of maturation placed her in an environmental situation that imposes demands upon her which she is not yet ready to meet.

Although, in theory, the ideal solution to such a situation is to gear the social demands and the social experiences of the individual to the level of his emotional maturation, in practice this ideal is not easy to attain. Placing the emotionally advanced child with a group chronologically older does not solve the problem, both because his shorter living experience causes adjustment problems between him and older children, and because of intellectual disparity; intellectual development follows chronogical, more closely than emotional, age. The same discrepancies would occur if one were to attempt to place a less emotionally mature child with children whose emotional ages are equivalent but who are younger chronologically and intellectually. From a practical standpoint the solution at the present time probably lies in a recognition by adults of the individual differences in the rate of emotional maturation, and in their support of the child who varies from the norm. It is probable that, unless deep emotional problems exist, these children, if given adequate support during the period of being "different," will eventually find themselves in a world no longer alien. The child whose maturation has been rapid will find that his chronological peer group finally catches up with him. The child whose emotional maturation has been slow will, in all probability, reach maturity; it simply takes him longer to get there. The problem can become complicated if adults fail to accept the variations in rate of maturation and therefore do not give support to the individual as he struggles both with his "alienness" to his peer group and his inability to comply with the demands made by a society that considers the average to be normal.

The difference in the average rate of maturation of boys and girls creates another social problem. The girl of fourteen is usually psychologically more mature than the boy of fourteen. This difference in emotional maturity is apparent in the social group. Adolescents themselves are aware of it and indicate it in their social behavior. The freshman high school girl does not usually find the freshman boy interesting, but is interested in older boys. The sophomore or junior high school boy prefers to date the freshman girl rather than a girl in his own class. Parents and teachers often become alarmed at these choices and attempt to press the young people to be interested in their own age group. If left to his own devices, the adolescent will tend to seek the companionship of the opposite sex in terms of his emotional rather than his chronological age. Although clinical experience shows that with certain individuals the choice of such companionship may be determined by neurotically colored motivations, more frequently it is determined by true compatibility. Thus, it is not alarming if a girl chooses a boy chronologically older than herself unless there is other evidence that this choice is motivated by unresolved conflicts. Again, in view of the difference in rate of maturation, it should also not be assumed that, because a boy and girl of the same chronological age are interested in each other, the choice is an indication of some emotional disturbance. It may only be an indication that the boy's rate of maturation has been more rapid or the spurt of growth has occurred earlier than would be anticipated from the statistically established norms.

An answer to the question, "Is it normal?" when applied to any behavior, lies in an accurate evaluation of the level of the emotional maturation of the particular adolescent. Unfortunately, we have no techniques for such accurate evaluation. Normality can only be approximated. Chronological age should not be the only yardstick; careful study of the developmental history and an evaluation of the present behavior in relation to it are probably the best means of judging the significance of behavior at any given time. Furthermore, it is important that the perspective that results from observation of any individual be gained before the personality structure is definitively evaluated. One should not attempt such a formulation until careful observation has been made of all aspects of the individual's reaction to his life situation. The evaluation should not be in terms of how he reacts one day to a particular situation. Detailed observation of an adolescent, covering his reactions to all situations in one day, must be combined with the consideration of his reactions to these situations at other times. A proper study of an adolescent must show him, not in a static portrait, but in action projected onto a movie screen.

IV. Social Adaptation

PARENTS, TEACHERS, AND GROUP WORKERS, in their day-by-day work with adolescents, observe certain characteristics that should be considered in developing a theoretical frame of reference for understanding the psychology of adolescence. Their observations attest to the variability and inconsistency of the youth of today. The psychological meaning of the apparent contradictions deserves scrutiny.

Independence and Dependence

The adolescent struggles for independence, verbalizing vehemently his protest against the protective ruling of the adult group. He does not want to be told what clothes to wear, what hours to keep, what food to eat, what political party to respect, or what ethical or moral formula to embrace. On the other hand, he is unable to handle his independent activities as adequately as he did in the immediate past. He is impulsive in his behavior and confused about his goals. Not only does this disturb the adults who are interested in his present and future adjustment; it also disturbs and frightens him. As a result, he is apt to make demands for dependence which he has not made since he was a small child. At the same time he wants advice about what clothes to wear, what hours to keep, what food to eat, what political party to respect, or what ethical or moral formula to embrace.

SOCIAL ADAPTATION

The Peer Group

The peer group dominates the adolescent's thinking and his behavior. Deliberately to violate peer group patterns is extremely difficult for him. The peer group is perhaps more difficult to define at this age than at any other period of development or periods of growth plateaus. The peer group is composed of individuals at approximately the same emotional level of development. It is not primarily determined by chronological age or intellectual ability, although both play a part. While superficially its influence may seem to be effected through the dominance of its key members (for example, Mary is a "big wheel," John is a "big shot"), the deeper cohesive force is, for most of its members, the mutual emotional empathy that exists. Excessively insecure individuals may seek membership in an incompatible peer group, but they imitate the members in order to gain status. They tend to remain on the fringe of the group. True members are a more inherent part of the group.

The carving on the escutcheon of the peer group reads: "One just doesn't do that." The motto supplies the answer to almost any question, whether it involves wearing a hat to town, straightening bobby socks so they are neater, wearing blue jeans that still retain their original color, being sexually promiscuous, or cheating in examinations.

In spite of the iron control of the peer group, membership is not lifetime. Exclusion from the peer group will occur if the member proves recalcitrant. The member may also voluntarily withdraw if his rate of emotional development proves at variance with that of the membership as a whole. During periods of marked fluctuation in the individual's degree of maturation, he may have loyalty to more than one peer group. He will then use the standards of the particular group that is at the moment most compatible with his emotional state, swinging with little hesitation to another group as the rise or fall in his maturity level influences his needs and his capacities.

Parents may complain that their son is easily influenced by the group with whom he happens to be. They will frequently say, "He has a group of friends who are such nice, mature boys. When he is with them he is fine. Then he becomes interested in another group for a few days. That group is rough, coarse, and unreliable. When he is with them he acts just like they do." This is true. Two factors are playing a part. Their son is controlled by each group with whom he is sharing an experience but, it must be remembered, he is with each group because of some, perhaps relatively temporary, empathy with them. He vacillates between contrasting peer groups because his needs vary.

Sexual Patterns

The adolescent's behavior toward the opposite sex is extremely confusing to those who observe it. A boy may appear excessively preoccupied with his relationship to girls, neglecting all other responsibilities in his attempt to fulfil what he sees as the demands of that interest. Then he may suddenly change his point of focus, centering his interest on boys; girls then either do not exist or are unworthy of his time. He is either occupied with seemingly purposeless activities with other boys or is engrossed in organized athletics. He may become devoted to a very desirable girl, at which point his parents relax because "he is finally showing some sense." Suddenly he may lose all interest in this desirable love object and choose, for the purpose of his social activities, a girl who is in complete contrast to the standards of his family and of the community. He may explain his abandonment of the first love object by stating that she is too nice. He explains his abandonment of the second by indicating that she is not nice enough. His loyalty to his peer group does not necessarily carry over to loyalty toward a girl with whom he has temporarily been compatible. He may talk freely about her in an extremely derogatory way, exaggerating her faults and denying her virtues. The problems created by the relationship may have been of such intensity that they neutralized the strength of his usual pattern of loyalty.

Interpersonal Relationships

The adolescent's manifest relationships with other people are extremely hard to classify. One moment he may hate intensely; the next, he may love with equal intensity. The object of his emotional response may be the same person or it may be a dif-

SOCIAL ADAPTATION

ferent person. The intensity of the response is not always consistent with the actual episode that aroused the reaction. At times he will forgive his boy friend who stole his girl friend. At another time he will swear everlasting enmity because his boy friend spoke disparagingly of a necktie. He may accept a severe but unjustified reprimand with a graciousness and tolerance that embarrass his harassed teacher. The next day he may show extreme rage because the same teacher asks him very patiently to try to write more legibly.

Contradictions in Verbalization and Behavior

The adolescent's verbalizations and his actual behavior are frequently, from day to day, contradictory. On occasion he verbalizes ideals, but any similarity between these ideals and his actual behavior is purely coincidental. On another occasion he may deny verbally all ideals. At this time his behavior may be in complete conformity with socially acceptable standards. Today he may idealize a certain philosophy of life, only to express tomorrow a slave-like devotion to a completely contrasting approach to the problems of living. At one time he follows too rigidly an idealized code of conduct, the demands of which, if really met, would deny him all human gratifications. As if by a sudden metamorphosis of character he then violates—or more often talks of violating—every acceptable code of behavior. To add to the confusion, but also to introduce a more optimistic note, it should be pointed out that the average adolescent, while never as angelic as he talks of being in his angelic moments, rarely acts out the extremes of anti-social behavior that he proclaims he wishes to adopt.

Parent Relationships

In no area is the adolescent's dichotomy more evident than in his relationship to his parents. At times he rejects his parents as if they were lepers in a community of healthy people. They dress too well or not well enough. They talk too loudly or not loudly enough. They are either martyrs or completely thoughtless. They know nothing or they know too much. In almost the next breath he reveals his idealization of them, picturing them as more saintly than the saints, more learned than the sages, more omnipotent than God. When he is in this phase, parents can do no wrong; their mistakes are met with sympathetic tolerance and understanding of the underlying motivations. The parents have the gratifying experience of finding someone who understands what a hard life they have had as parents and as adults. It is extremely confusing for parents to deal with a child who has shown gracious understanding of their whim to indulge themselves in the use of the family car for pleasure, but who later responds with a vitriolic attack when they plan to use the car for a necessary errand.

Secretiveness and Self-Revelation

The adolescent characteristically is secretive about himself and his feelings. Most of the time it is extremely difficult for him to verbalize how he does feel. Futhermore, he is timorous about exposing himself to others even if he can put his feelings into words. Again, however, this pattern is not consistent. Suddenly he may bare his soul (or so it seems), revealing his ambitions, his feelings of guilt, and his conscious awareness of the nature of many of the conflicts with which he is struggling. Sometimes this revelation is a frank one but limited by the degree of his own insight. At other times it is probably consciously or unconsciously distorted. Percival M. Symonds analyzes material he obtained from three sources: the evaluations made by others of individual adolescents, the adolescents' own self-evaluations, and personality evaluations made through projective tests.[1] This material shows clearly the contrast between an individual adolescent as seen by others, as seen consciously by himself, and as seen in an analysis of his personality structure.

Undoubtedly, adolescents frequently distort the verbal picture they give of their feelings. One girl expressed this rather interestingly. She stated that she often confided in her mother, discussing with her mother some of the problems that she was facing in her attempt to adjust to her status of an embryonic adult. She stated, however, that what she discussed was carefully selected.

[1] Percival M. Symonds, *Adolescent Fantasy*, Columbia University Press, New York, 1949.

She felt that certain stages preceded her verbalization to her mother. The first stage was a feeling of general confusion, in which she found herself thinking such contradictory thoughts, with the contradictions occurring so rapidly, that she was unable to formulate sharply the nature of the contradictions. During this period she remained silent. Gradually some of the contradictions took on sharper form. She was then able to think in terms of these contradictions and to develop from them a definite point of view. During this period, again, she did not talk to her mother because she did not wish to be influenced by her mother's attitudes. Finally, the particular subject about which she was in conflict became clear enough to her so that she could find her own definite answer. She then felt that she knew what concepts she wished to abandon in order to accept others.

In other words, in a particular area of concious conflict, this girl had developed a philosophy of approach. She would then discuss her particular question with her mother, but would not present her own conclusions. She reviewed with her mother the various solutions of which she had thought. If her mother suggested a solution other than the one she herself had found, she attempted to evaluate it frankly and test her own solution against the one her mother offered. If her mother's solution seemed sounder, she might change. More frequently she either would win her mother to her own point of view or would become angry at her mother for her obvious stupidity. This particular mother was extremely proud of the close relationship she had with her daughter, being quite certain that she was the recipient of genuine confidences from her daughter.

Joan, another adolescent, gave a slightly different version of what confiding in parents can mean for some adolescents. Joan was receiving psychiatric treatment for prophylactic reasons rather than because of any deep disturbance. She told the psychiatrist that she had given some advice to Mary, a friend of hers, and wished the psychiatrist's opinion of its soundness. She then told the following story. About two o'clock in the morning, Mary, who was in tears, had called her. Mary had gone to bed after returning from a date but was awakened by her mother, who was crying. When Mary questioned her mother as to the cause of this disturbance, the mother said that Mary did not love her, that she could not bear living because she felt that Mary was indifferent to her. She was planning, within the next few days, after everything was straightened out, to commit suicide. Mary had attempted to console her mother by assuring her that she did love her. She joined her mother in a tearful scene, and finally persuaded her mother to go to bed. Later she called Joan for advice.

Joan pointed out to Mary that she was directly responsible for this episode; she had made many mistakes in the way she handled her mother. For example, when she came in from a date she did not awaken her mother, because her mother was tired and sleeping. When she talked about her date with her mother, she never went further than to say she had a good time. She never talked to her mother about things that girls might be disturbed about. Joan had quite different recommendations in regard to proper management of mothers. She suggested that when Mary came home she should awaken her mother, asking her to talk with her. If the mother accepted the invitation, the next step was clear. If the mother refused, Mary should find an opportunity to tell her mother that she was hurt by the rebuff, that she wanted to talk over some things that were worrying her. If necessary, she should force her mother to listen to a tale of woe. Mary should tell her mother she was worried about some feelings she had; for example, that she was frightened by the feelings she had when a boy kissed her, or by the implications of getting married.

To all this advice, Mary said, "But Joan, I don't want my mother to know how I feel and what bothers me; she would be horrified. She would give me platitudes and call them advice. She would only irritate me." Joan's answer was, "But Mary, you don't see the point. You don't talk to your mother about the things that really bother you. You tell her that you are bothered by things that don't disturb you. Then, whatever she says won't make any difference to you. Your mother will feel happier and she'll think you love her; she won't commit suicide. You know, there are lots of things that people think girls of our age should be bothered about that you are not bothered about at all. Those are the things to talk to your mother about." It would certainly appear that Joan herself had worked out an approach to her mother that keeps her mother happy and Joan's secrets still secret.

SOCIAL ADAPTATION

The Meaning of the Inconsistency

These observations about adolescents by no means cover all the possible variations that could be presented. They are perhaps sufficient, however, to indicate a universal characteristic of the normal adolescent. He is always a contradiction. Few characteristics observed today can be counted upon to influence his behavior tomorrow. These contradictions are the result of his attempt to find clear-cut answers to internal conflicts and to problems that his reality world imposes upon him. They are attempts to lock out one part of this conflict in order to fulfil the urges that the contrasting part of the conflict activates. He is attempting to avoid discord by choosing a variety of notes to play singly. He does not know how to play several notes in harmony.

The significant stimulus for the confused behavior of the adolescent is undoubtedly the biological change that occurs at this time. This biological change, which manifests itself so clearly in the modification of the body structure, has an equally strong impact upon the psychological equilibrium of the individual. As was pointed out in Chapter II, the first manifestation of the psychological change is probably an increased pressure toward maturation. Very shortly, however, this general urge toward maturation is increased and complicated by an increase in the sexual drive. It would seem that, along with the increased urgency for maturation and the more specific urgency for sexual fulfilment, there is a concomitant increase in aggressive energy with which to strike out more effectively against controlling forces that strive to prevent gratification of impulses.

These three phases of the psychological structure of the individual are closely interrelated. Increased energy to face life situations more aggressively is essential for fulfilment of the incentive toward maturation. The most significant development toward psychological maturation at this age is the gradual acceptance of heterosexual orientation and gratification. Thus, whatever may be the first manifestation of adolescence, very shortly the more aggressive attack upon life problems, the striving for maturation, and the struggle for heterosexual adjustment become fused into the so-called typical behavior of the adolescent. The psychological structure of the adolescent is the composite result of the multiple aspects of this process. The psychological structure develops within the framework of his past patterns of adjustment, the demands of his present needs, the demands of the society he lives in, and the pressure to reach the nebulous, but demanding, goal he has for the future. In order to understand the adolescent psychologically, the significance of his past must be studied, the dynamics of his present must be evaluated, and his goals, both nebulous and practical, must be clarified.

and having abandoned his struggle to become adult. This is a real blow to his pride. He resents his dependency because it has threatened his confidence in himself as a potential adult. In order to maintain his own self-respect, he must protest against this flight into childhood. To protest against himself is to acknowledge his own weakness, which he wishes to deny. He seeks a victim outside himself upon whom to vent his anger, since by being angry at another he denies his disappointment in and his anger at himself. He chooses for his attack those who were cognizant of his defeat—his parents or other adults. He protests angrily that they will not let him grow up; they treat him as a child. He has chosen to be angry at his parents as a means of denying his own weakness and in order to shelter himself from his own self-contempt.

If, on the other hand, the parents do not respond to the adolescent's regressive demands, his anxiety mounts. He may then turn upon the parents, angrily accusing them of expecting too much of him. Again the parents are accused of failure so that he may avoid his own sense of defeat.

A situation fraught with danger to the ultimate maturation of the adolescent is one in which he cannot express a need for both dependence and independence and thus gain gratification in transient phases of each. This danger is present if the adolescent is unwilling to indulge himself in dependent gratification or to expose himself to experimental independence. Dependency may be too tempting and thus must be denied. The need, however, may be denied because past experience has taught him that he will either be rebuffed or permanently engulfed by these adults. Independence may, in contrast, be too overwhelming because his past experience has not given him confidence in his own resources or in his ability to use them. He may also be quite willing to accept gratification for his contrasting longings for freedom and protection, only to find his environment unwilling either to accept his desire to be free or to satisfy his desire to be protected.

Undoubtedly, it is true that many times the complaint the adolescent makes concerning his parents is valid; they may not give support when they should and may refuse freedom of choice when he should have it. It is important, however, that the situation be evaluated carefully. The adolescent's description of any single situation is not always an accurate appraisal of parental attitudes. Diagnostic conclusions should not be reached without more information than that obtained from a description by the adolescent of one emotionally charged episode. The normal parent of the normal adolescent inevitably is frequently in the opposite phase from that which the adolescent desires. If the parent is fulfilling one need, the opposing need of the adolescent often becomes dominant. If the parent is meeting the adolescent's dependency needs, the adolescent will sooner or later gain the security that makes possible a rebellion against that dependency. If the parent is giving adequate freedom to the adolescent, the latter will expose himself to situations that are frightening and he will wish to return to a childlike relationship for a time. He will usually save his self-respect by blaming the parent for advising him either too much or too little.

A chronically frightened adolescent is a disturbed adolescent. Broadly speaking, either his earlier experiences have not given him an optimum background of security and tools adequate to deal with the present reality, or else the present reality is, for some reason peculiar to him and his surroundings, too overwhelming for him to master. On the other hand, in the author's experience, the adolescent who does not indicate some conflict over his strivings to become independent should be studied carefully. Perhaps he *has* found a way through adolescence which has not been too frightening. It is also possible that the struggle is there but is carefully hidden. The problems presented at the onset of adolescence may have been too overwhelming for the child and, under a thin façade of growing up, he actually has remained fixed at a younger, more comfortable level of adjustment. Just as it is impossible to go from one place to another without some path covering the intervening distance, an individual cannot go from childhood to adulthood without being adolescent. Either he stays in childhood or he weathers adolescence.

Ambivalence in the Adolescent

The ambivalence of adolescents toward people to whom they are close has many characteristics of the anxiety-ridden ambivalence of early childhood. There is also considerable similarity in the etiology of this behavior. About the time the child learns to walk, to talk, and is accepting more or less the demands of toilet training, he often manifests psychological disturbances. He may become anxious, expressing his anxiety through daytime fears or night terrors. He may also show irritability and resentment toward his parents. He has discovered new worlds to conquer and new capacities in himself with which to conquer them, only to find that many of these new opportunities are forbidden by parents. The child resents the restrictions imposed. He expresses this resentment in hostility toward the parents. This hostility frightens the child because of fear that it will result in the destruction of the parents' love if not of the parents themselves. If, on the other hand, he accepts the restrictions in order to hold parental love and protects the parents from his own hostility, he faces an unbearable frustration resulting from lack of gratification of his own desires. It appears that the price he must pay to be secure in his love relationship with his parents is the relinquishment of all other wishes. The price of fulfilment of his wishes is a relinquishment of the security and gratification that lie in the love his parents offer him. The child finally resolves this conflict. He gradually realizes that his hostility kills neither his parents nor his parents' love, so that it is safe to hate a love object. He finds substitute outlets that are permissible. He develops skills that make it possible for him to engage in previously forbidden behavior.

At adolescence the surge of new impulses and invigorated older drives places the individual in a comparably frustrating situation. Parents impose limitations on many types of gratification, limitations which are frustrating but which are more or less obeyed in order to avoid the anxiety that parental disapproval would cause. The adolescent has a great deal of disorganized energy which adults would like him to channelize toward constructive goals. He, having not yet determined his goals, wishes to express the energy impulsively as it mounts. He is noisy, rushes around in a disorganized fashion, laughs loudly, is often clumsy, talks too loudly, sings too often, and forgets his manners. He wants the car right now, a new suit right now, something to eat right now. The logic behind a restriction imposed seems irrelevant and unimportant when stacked against the strong emotional force behind the impulse.

Adolescents make many illogical demands and wish to carry out plans of action that are incompatible with the social mores. Parents return to saying "no" and "don't" with a frequency that has its closest counterpart in their behavior during the very early toddling age of the child. The adolescent, his energy restrained and his whims not gratified, resents the source of his discomfort—adults. His feelings are too raw and too intense to be handled either with diplomacy to gain external acceptance, or with rationalization to achieve internal comfort. He hates his parents.

This hatred is no safer than it was in childhood. He needs parental love as intensely as he has ever needed it. Moreover, he has, through the course of years, developed a real love for his parents. He is afraid to deny his love for and need for love from his parents. The resultant anxiety and guilt make hatred untenable. He reverses his emotions, loving his parents with the intensity with which he has hated them.

The sudden inability to handle love and hostility toward the same love object is reflected in his relationships with his friends. At times his need to be reassured that his friends accept him is dominant. He accepts their behavior toward him as if that acceptance were the price he pays to maintain his security. At other times he feels that the restrictions they impose upon him destroy him as an individual. He then fears their rejection and is angry that they demand so much of him. His answer is to hate them, hoping thus to be free of his need for them. At times friends may be critical of something which, superficially, seems relatively unimportant but, fundamentally, may be deeply significant as a symbol of a goal toward which he is striving. The criticism then undermines a structure that is much deeper than the obvious point of attack. The result is fear, with a defensive anger aroused to deny or overcome that fear. Friendship with a peer often has an obscure component—the role of substitute parent. As such, the friend may be exposed to the same ambivalent feeling that the adolescent expresses toward his parents.

Since the adolescent's feelings are too intense to be kept in balance by compromises, renunciation, and substitute gratifications, under stress he reveals the several facets of his emotional relationships with people as if they were separate entities. Under less stress he will respond with the reasonableness of his pre-adolescent days. Frequently, however, the intensity of his emotional response to a particular situation is of such magnitude that his

DEPENDENCY AND AMBIVALENCE

formerly established pattern for dealing with ambivalent feelings breaks down.

Gradually, the normal adolescent, if he finds he has not provoked a totally hostile response from his environment, will again find patterns of behavior with which to avoid chronic frustration. He finds substitute gratification for impulses that, in unsublimated form, cannot be gratified. The panic created by forced inhibition of his impulses is allayed by rationalization and by acceptance of over-all goals for himself, and he again becomes master of his ambivalence. His energy, recently expressed so explosively, once again becomes channelized. He settles down to his school work, organizes his social life, systematizes his living in the present, and recognizes and follows the guideposts that will lead him to his future goals.

As the adolescent develops a capacity to harmonize his multiple impulses, he again sets up his own controls. This mastery of impulses is a recapitulation of the earlier developmental period when he learned to say "no" to himself before his parents said it, thereby facilitating his adjustment to his internal demands and external restrictions. Again, during adolescence, the individual's behavior gradually is determined by his own permissiveness and his own restrictions rather than by controls imposed from outside. As a result, his parents and his friends are less frustrating and his hostility toward them lessens. The storms in interpersonal relationships, so frequently observed during the early phase of adolescence, decrease in frequency as he approaches psychological adulthood.

VI. Psychosexual Conflicts

WHILE THE ADOLESCENT IS STRUGGLING to gain security in the more broadly stimulating world that has been opened to him, and while he flounders in the sea of his ambivalent feelings and disorganized impulses, a major and more significant struggle, on a relatively unconscious level, is taking place within him. Additional ambiguities in his behavior, an intensification of his struggle for independence, and further confusion in his responses to his parents develop. This struggle has its basis in the multi-causal difficulties he faces as he strives to reach a heterosexual level of adjustment.

In order to understand the sexual problems of adolescence it is essential to understand the earlier sexual development of the child. As the small child develops capacity to deal with the insecurities of his environment and to find relative security therein, and as he finds a solution to his ambivalent feelings toward parent figures and the reality world about him, his emotional energy is not completely expended in meeting his immediate needs. A reservoir of emotional energy remains which finds an outlet in a new capacity to love as well as to seek love. There is probably a brief period in which this love is given indiscriminately. Very soon, however, the greater intensity of this love is directed toward the parent of the opposite sex. As a result, the parent of the same sex becomes a rival for the love and attention of the parent of the opposite sex. The classical family triangle comes into being.

During the oedipal phase the male child resents his father as a rival. This resentment, however, is dangerous since his adversary is obviously a more powerful person than himself. The boy assumes the father will react to a rival with the same hostility that he himself feels. Because of his father's greater strength the boy in fantasy sees himself threatened in the uneven struggle. As a result he may hate and fear his father. Usually he also loves his father. This love is a source of security to him, providing the satisfaction that comes from loving and being loved. He does not wish to renounce this gratification. He is, therefore, pressed for a solution of his conflict not only because of fear of his father but also because of his wish to maintain a positive relationship which in itself is gratifying.

The mother does not accept the boy as a competitor of the father. She sees him as her child, the father as her husband. The boy, therefore, faces a real threat to his confidence in himself; not only is he unable to destroy his father, but even were his father destroyed, his mother would not reward his victory by allowing him to displace his father in her affections. He recognizes his own inadequacy, which is more than his mere inability to overcome his father. He is aware that in the eyes of his mother he is inadequate as a masculine figure.

In an attempt to solve this multiphase conflict the little boy takes several significant steps. He renounces his infantile sexual aims and represses the basic structure of his rivalry with his father by denying its sexual aspects. Having abandoned a sexual goal, he then is free to strive to be like the father. The rationale for this attempted identification is obvious. If he is like his father he may then gain his father's approval. Furthermore, if he is like his father—since the latter seems to be the type of person his mother loves—he will be secure in his mother's love. He accepts his father as an ideal on which to pattern himself, a safe pattern so long as he abandons his attempted sexual rivalry with his father and does not seek sexual recognition from his mother. In addition, he recognizes that, in his mother's eyes, his father is not perfect —in certain areas he might be improved upon. He therefore strives subtly to continue his attack on his earlier adversary. As long as he represses the sexual motivation that was the original reason for his inevitable defeat, he may cement his relationship with his mother by striving to be the type of masculine figure she appears to hold in greatest esteem. Therefore, his ego-ideal, while predominantly patterned by identification with his father, is also colored by the implied concept of his mother's ideal of a man. With the acceptance of a masculine identification but with desexualized goals, the little boy develops a pattern of behavior which defines his role in a bisexual world.

While attempting to handle the conflicts inherent in the family relationships, he also relieves the intensity of the emotional struggle by seeking to dilute the concentration of the love which he has until now focused on the family. He turns part of it toward less conflicting love objects. He seeks emotional gratification through relationships with his peer group and with adults outside the family circle. This is possible when in his past experience he found reason to believe that not only his parents but people in general are a source of security to him in the world beyond the family constellation. In turning to friends of his own age and to parent substitutes outside his family circle, he begins the long process of socialization. Developmentally, he has entered "latency."

Sexual Conflicts of the Adolescent Boy

The physical changes of puberty bring an intensification of the biologically determined sexual drive. The mechanisms of repression utilized during the earlier childhood period are no longer adequate against the strengthened drive. Sexual impulses threaten to break through the earlier established barriers. If this occurred in relation to a new love object, the problem would be less severe. It does not do so. Although the pathway established in handling earlier sexual impulses has become covered with camouflaging overgrowth, it still is the only familiar road to follow once the barrier is down. The sexuality of early adolescence reactivates the family triangle, and the boy's mother becomes the focus of his sexual feelings. Expression of this is forbidden by previously determined prohibitions; yet the need for expression is intensified. New defenses must be established in order to strengthen the protective repression. The defense most likely to have the strength to combat the newly intensified impulses is that of denial of the outlet that is sought. The adolescent boy denies the appeal his mother has.

Clinically, the boy's need to avoid an affectionate relationship with his mother is easily recognized. Although he had in the past accepted his mother's physical manifestations of affection, he now refuses to accept them. His mother, he insists, not only must refrain from kissing him; she must avoid all physical contact with him. Verbal expressions of affection on her part are met with annoyance. If she praises him, he protests that she is treating him "like a baby."

If the mother hazards a suggestion as to how her son should act, he responds with irritation, even when the suggestion coincides with his own plans. Not only is her suggestion about his behavior met by refusal, but often it results in behavior of an opposite nature. This rebuff is necessary to reassure himself that he is capable of independent action, free from the dictates of his mother. He can then reiterate to himself that he is not the sort of person his mother wishes him to be. The adolescent boy must belittle and avoid following the mother's concept of masculinity. The weakening defenses against infantile sexual goals and the indentification with the mother's concept of masculinity, which entered into his original solution of the family triangle, make such tactics necessary. Identification and acceptance of the mother's ideal of a man as a model for his own masculinity were safe only so long as the sexual implications of the relationship were repressed. With the weakening of his defenses against the sexual nature of the relationship, identification with and acceptance of her concept of a man becomes too dangerous. Should he succeed in emulating the masculine figure she admires, he exposes himself to the possibility of becoming her love object and seducing her. This forbidden aim must be denied.

It is interesting to speculate about why a simple prohibition imposed upon a small child by his father's presence takes on the nature of a taboo in adolescence. The explanation lies in part in the intensity of the impulses and, to the child, in the grave dangers of expressing these impulses. Direct exposure to such a painful struggle must be avoided. The universality of the taboo against incest suggests that this prohibition is inherent in the human race. At any rate, by the time the individual has reached adolescence, he has been exposed to society's condemnation of incest. Certain non-sexual aspects of the boy's relationship with his mother may also contribute to his denial of sexual feelings directed toward her. Of necessity, she has been a dominating, prohibiting person who, whether she used it or not, always had the power to administer severe punishment. By implication, therefore, such a love object would not only restrain the boy from reaching independence but would also be a love object capable of punitive action.

Experience in the past, in relationship to the mother, had an effect upon the boy's evaluation of himself. In childhood, sexual aims toward the mother exposed the boy to the discomfiture of facing his own inadequacy; she did not accept him as a love object. To seek her again would be to expose himself to further rebuff. Feelings of inadequacy and of anxiety which are rooted in the difficulty he experiences in establishing himself as an adult are augmented by the attitude his mother takes toward him. A mother may be relatively immune to the charms of her adolescent son and continue to see him as a son rather than a lover. This attitude, while sexually more comfortable for the boy, accentuates his sense of inferiority. She not only ignores him as a sexual object, but implies that he is only a child. Another mother may respond to the sexual maturation of her son and unconsciously, if not consciously, try to seduce him into a disguised sexual relationship. Her overtures are extremely frightening to the boy since they expose him to his incestuous longings. He senses that if he is to mature, he must escape this pitfall. That all boys do not escape is obvious when one considers the number of men who have remained over-attached to their mothers.

Regardless of the nature of his relationship to his mother, the boy must abandon that part of his ideal for himself which had its roots in his mother's standards, if he is to attain heterosexual and social maturity. The sexual implication of accepting his mother's image of an ideal man to emulate can no longer be tolerated, because of the increased intensity of his own sexuality. With the internal pressure for his own maturation, he cannot solve the problem by remaining a sexually repressed little boy. He therefore must place a value on those attributes that conflict with her concepts of masculinity.

The part of the child's ideal formerly colored by his identification with his father now becomes equally hazardous. If he is like his father, he is again the type of man of whom his mother approves and thus he exposes himself to the danger of winning his mother's love in competition with his father. But another and new danger also exists. Previously, accepting this ideal served in part as a means of assuring himself of his father's love. Love now is too sexually dominated. If he values his father's love he faces the danger of his sexuality finding expression in his relationship with his father, an unacceptable outlet. He is driven, then, to avoid this danger by denying that part of his ideal rooted in his identification with his father.

This need to deny the sexual significance of identification with the father is not isolated from the implications of identification which are related to the boy's need to achieve independence and dignity. Mimicry of his father means to the boy that he is inadequate. Achievement of mature behavior, patterned after his father's, represents only a shell that covers fundamental weaknesses. While he has an exaggerated feeling of inadequacy during this period, the urge toward maturation carries with it an implication of his own potential worth. While on the one hand he fears he cannot achieve maturity on his own, he also cherishes the contradictory conviction that he can. He does not wish to abandon his hope by covering up his former fear through mimicry. Thus, he wishes to prove himself an independent individual by abandoning that part of the ideal which reflects his imitation of his father.

The adolescent boy utilizes another defense against his sense of inadequacy. His feelings of fear and incompetence, which were aroused in the earlier period of competition with his father but remained dormant, are now reawakened by the reactivation of the triangular emotional constellation. He must deny his father's strength and attractiveness in order to conceive of himself as a more powerful male figure. He establishes his own self-respect by denying the virtues of his adversary. He belittles his father—in thought, in action, and in words. Also, his mother's refusal to accept him as a sexual object may again confront him if he over-extends himself. In order to avoid the feeling of inadequacy that this fantasied rebuff would bring, he must deny the sexuality of his mother. She fails to accept him, then, not because he is inadequate but because she is incapable of sexual response. His father is a nincompoop, his mother a hag.

With a brave gesture the adolescent has stripped his parents of their powers to obstruct him and has cleared the way for his own sexual and social maturation. He is free, but his sense of freedom is short-lived. Stripping his parents of their power, he finds he has inadvertently disarmed himself as well. Instead of finding adequacy he has increased his own inadequacy. The edifice of his maturation which he has been erecting was not structured by happenstance. The bricks that fitted together to lay the foundation for his character were molded from forms designed by the parents. Removing the individual bricks now threatens to destroy all he has built. His ego-ideal, which included his own concept of his father as a man as well as his mother's ideal of desirable masculinity, cannot be so easily overthrown. By accepting, as his own, the standards of behavior acceptable to his mother and father, he felt safe in the world of his family in early childhood. The application of these standards proved relatively effective in his broader social world. The patterns of behavior that resulted from emulating his parents and living up to his ego-ideal provided a comfortable, successful, and reassuringly consistent reaction to life situations. Abandonment of his ideal results in a deep sense of loss. He then no longer has the assurance that he is able to deal comfortably, automatically, and successfully with the demands of the reality world. He has stripped himself of tools that he had learned to use. He has abandoned relative sureness for complete uncertainty.

If he seeks to fill the vacuum he created when he renounced his identification with his father, by returning to an acceptance of the security inherent in being like his father, he then must face the significance of the denial of his father's strength. If he is like his father he will be as inadequate as he wishes to believe his father is. Identification with his father will no longer cause him to feel adequate in the world, for he has convinced himself that his father is weak. By attempting to enhance his own relative strength, he belittled his father. Now he finds that in belittling his father he has belittled that part of himself which contributed significantly to his sense of security. If he is not like his father, he has no standard to follow. If he is like his father, he is, by his own definition, a nincompoop.

His denial of the role his mother has played in his life adds further to his confusion. If his relationship with his mother has been a satisfactory, though asexual, one in the past, his ideal of femininity derives from the satisfaction and security he found in his relationship with her. Thus, his ultimate image of a heterosexual love object would be someone like his mother. In order to win such a love object, the most obvious answer is to become like his father, with the modifications suggested by his mother's picture of the ideal man. He cannot abandon this composite idea of a man if he is to gain the love object he seeks. Also, if he denies the sexual potentiality of his mother, he equally denies that of his ideal love object. How can he be sure of gratification for his total love needs if he accepts the serious limitations he has placed on his ideal man and ideal woman?

Clinically, we can differentiate between these confusions. In one phase the adolescent boy refuses his mother's affection and renounces her concepts of masculinity. He ridicules his father and struggles to be indiscriminately "different." His parents' concepts of how he should dress, what he should believe politically, and how he should act socially are of value only negatively; they indicate what one should *not* believe or do. The parents dress wrong, have embarrassing table manners, act wrong, and talk wrong. They are completely impossible. In the alternate phase he seeks the mother's response provocatively, flirting with her as if she had suddenly lost her scars of age and had become an attractive adolescent herself. He accepts his father as an oracle and treats him as if he were the exceptional man he always wished him to be. The boy seeks advice on every move, as if he were incapable of independent judgment; he is again the helpless child of infancy.

Sexual Conflicts of the Adolescent Girl

The adolescent girl faces an identical struggle except that the mother is the rival and model, the father the ideal, but forbidden, sexual object. While she feels drawn toward the father, she must deny this attraction. Yet she cannot judge other men with confidence except by standards calibrated according to her concept of her father. She does not dare to be like her mother; she must deny her mother's virtues in order to assure herself of her own superiority to her mother. Yet her clearest definition of femininity is that with which her mother has acquainted her, and which she has accepted as a model for herself. She vacillates between contempt for her mother and father, idealization of her mother and father, contempt for her father and idealization of her mother, idealization of her father and contempt for her mother.

Actually, the situation is more difficult for the average girl than it is for the average boy. There are two chief contributory factors in this greater difficulty, stemming in part from experiences in the early years of the girl's life. In infancy the mother is the chief source of security to both the boy and the girl. The little boy does not jeopardize this security in his relationship with his mother, as he faces the problems of the family triangle, to the same extent as does the little girl. The little girl, in becoming a rival to her mother, exposes herself to the danger of depriving herself of emotional security. She fears that her mother will withdraw her love in retaliation if she—the girl—presumes to be a rival for the father's attention. The regression that occurs when the adolescent girl is faced with situations that overwhelm her results in a need for a protective, dependent relationship with her mother. If she becomes a sexual person she fears that her mother will withdraw her support, just as she feared the same reaction during the earlier period of life. Thus, while the boy fears to reveal his sexuality because he may then be in danger from both his mother and his father, the degree of danger appears somewhat greater to the girl. She has more to lose in becoming the sexual rival of the parent of the same sex than the boy does.

In our culture the girl has further difficulty in her identification with her mother, as she strives to fulfil her role as a mature woman. Our culture, on the whole, does not provide a milieu that is conducive to the fulfilment of the normal biological urges of women. Too often a woman finds that biological fertility results in sterility in other aspects of her life. It is as if an excellent cake were covered with a bitter or tasteless frosting. As a consequence, many women fail to find a desirable and adequate means of self-fulfilment. Some hate being women and strive to deny their femininity. They attempt to belittle or deny their biological goal in order to avoid the frustrations of other aspects of their personality if their biological role is fulfilled. They imply to their daughters that to succumb to the temptation of being a wife and mother is to expose oneself to slavery under an indifferent, if not a cruel, master. Other women destroy their multiple potentialities by equating femininity with parasitical living. They then claim that their other potentials were actually artifacts, or that their talents were allowed to atrophy as the price they paid for biological expression. Some women are martyrs to their biological and social roles, viewing ther femininity and its cultural demands as a cross to be borne. Their destructiveness toward themselves and others makes them, like all martyrs, difficult to endure. If the mother has not found rich and multiple gratification in her own femininity, identification with the mother inevitably creates a conflictual struggle for the girl. The identification may lead to an unsatisfactory distortion of inherent feminine drives; it may lead to relinquishment of other drives; or it may lead to predominance of other drives at the price of repression of the biologically structured psychological role of femininity.

Although the problem of the girl in identifying with the mother who herself has failed to find a desirable role as a woman is more common than that of the boy in his identification with his father, attention should be called to the fact that in some cases the boy actually faces a similiar situation. A man does not inevitably find a satisfactory outlet for his masculinity any more than a woman inevitably finds one for her femininity. The social structure of our culture superficially appears to provide a richer role for the man. Whether this is basically true is subject to question. The current joke in which the woman says, "Sure, this is a man's world—women are too sensible to want it," may not be as humorous as it appears at first sight. For many reasons, the complete fulfilment of normal human drives is not always psychologically or socially possible. Drives that are possibly characteristic of masculine biological urges may suffer the same fate that biologically determined feminine drives often do. Individuals, whether they are men or women, will vary in their ability to handle the psychological, physiological, and social pressures with which they are faced. As a result, the boy may, in his identification with his father, experience the same confusion, the same frustration as the girl. His father may present to him a pattern for identification which will result in just as serious a distortion of his total personality structure as the mother may provide for the girl. The urge in any individual adolescent toward biological, psychological, and sociological maturity, in general, will be handicapped to the extent that the adolescent's object of identification is inadequate. Heterosexual maturity implies a successful transfer of feelings originally directed toward the parent of the opposite sex to a love object that is not taboo. Equally importantly, it implies a capacity for emotional gratification in the biologically determined role to which the individual was born.

VII. The Fate of the Conscience

DURING ADOLESCENCE A STRUGGLE with the conscience occurs. The conscience develops in early childhood and reaches a discernible form at the time of the resolution of the conflicts centering in the family triangle. The conscience is the result of the incorporation into the child's unconscious psychological structure of the standards imposed by the parents. The child is thereby enabled to avoid the danger of rejection or punishment by the parents. He assumes a role previously carried by his parents, becoming his own monitor and disciplinarian.

In Freud's formulation of the concept of the superego—or conscience—he states that the superego may be subsequently modified.[1] The child is influenced by other adults as well as by siblings and other children. Clinical observation of children during the latency period indicates that a modification does occur. At this period, certain prohibitions imposed by the parent and incorporated into the formulation of the conscience are abandoned. As the child seeks gratification from social contacts outside the family, he finds himself exposed to the rejection or punishment of his group if he does not accept certain standards that may be in addition or contradictory to those of his family.

Cleanliness is a simple example of this change. Parents' standards imposed during the early period of the child's life, if unmodified, would result in every boy's being an immaculate and faultlessly

[1] Sigmund Freud, *An Outline of Psychoanalysis*, W. W. Norton & Co., New York, 1949, Chap. 1.

dressed Little Lord Fauntleroy. The group helps him to escape this fate by denying the value of cleanliness. Most parents accept this change without protest, seeing it as evidence of growing up. It is, however, a significant change. The child's unconscious attitude toward cleanliness is modified in order to achieve acceptance by the peer group. The modification of the superego during latency, and the role of the peer group in initiating the change, have real significance during adolescence.

Rebellion Against Infantile Conscience

A major psychological struggle in the process of maturation, which occurs in adolescence, is rebellion against the infantile conscience. The infantile conscience was adequate for the adjustment of a small child; its structure was determined by the needs and requirements of childhood. The same standards of adjustment are not satisfactory for adult living, and because the conscience is a part of childhood, it becomes a barrier against maturation. An adolescent feels he must free himself from infantile modes of behavior; he rebels against his own conscience.

This rebellion against his conscience plays a part in the determination of two characteristics of adolescence which are often alarming. The adolescent flaunts his new freedom from his conscience; he verbalizes his contempt for its demands and acts out token proof that he is free of it. In seeking a symbol of his conscience against which to strike, he most frequently chooses the persons who were the determinants of the original pattern for his conscience—his parents. A significant part of the adolescent's rebellion against parental control is actually a symbolic rebellion against the no longer serviceable part of his own unconscious demands upon himself.

If the structure of the infantile conscience is considered in detail, it becomes obvious why the adolescent must rebel against it. Heterosexuality is forbidden by the infantile conscience. It was the need to find an efficient means of repressing parent-forbidden impulses, especially the early sexual impulses directed toward the parent of the opposite sex, which resulted in the crystallization of the infantile conscience. The early sexual feelings were, in embryonic form, the beginning of ultimate adult heterosexuality. Sexual feelings must be freed of the chains by which they were bound in childhood before mature heterosexuality can be attained. Also, in other areas of development the conscience has imposed unwarranted restrictions. As the child moves into adulthood, activities, drives, and impulses that were forbidden to him as a small child now become permissible. To the infantile conscience, that which was once bad is always bad. It protests against any act that was forbidden in childhood and is deaf to the approval expressed by a more flexible reality world. This is true because of the nature of the repression that took place. It is characteristic of repressed drives and feelings that they remain unconscious but unchanged in structure and in power. The repressing force therefore tends also to remain unchanged in structure and in power. This concept, familiar in our understanding of the neuroses, is equally true in the psychological format of the so-called normal individual.

The rebellion against the conscience is frightening to the child. Previously the conscience gave the individual a sense of ease with himself. He felt assured that his impulses would not be expressed in a form that would jeopardize his security since the pattern was molded by internal standards that mirrored the demands of the external world. Impulses now strengthened by new energy are difficult to hold in check by former methods; whereas to abandon the protection of the former methods is to invite chaos. As the anxiety mounts, the adolescent has need to strengthen old defenses. The conscience then becomes more alert and more rigid than before. The adolescent becomes overly severe toward himself—a swing in the opposite direction from his earlier abandonment to impulsive behavior. The adolescent suddenly becomes a prig.

In one phase, the adolescent may be frighteningly free of inhibitions, and, in the alternate phase, may be deprived of all normal spontaneity by unrealistic, self-imposed prohibitions. A girl was referred to a psychiatrist because of her unconventional behavior which had resulted in her being branded as the "bad girl" of the community. Her dress, her mannerisms, and her verbalization seemed to flaunt her defiance of all conventional standards. When the psychiatrist, in a comment, implied that he thought she permitted boys to kiss her, she left treatment. As an adult she recalled this episode. She could remember her horror at the thought that the psychiatrist had so little respect for her decency that he would believe it possible that she behaved in this manner—a manner completely unacceptable to her.

The adolescent often handles this conflict between the wish to be free of the conscience and slavish devotion to it by verbalization of defiance but with complete compliance to standards in actual behavior. Sometimes, however, the defiance is not only verbal but is acted out, with serious consequences. Usually, then, the acting out that occurs during the phase of defiance results in an overwhelming guilt reaction when the conscience is again in control. The conscience did not succeed in prohibiting the behavior, but once the act is committed, it must use all its force to punish. Such behavior is difficult to evaluate, diagnostically, in adolescence. It resembles the clinical picture of adults who act out impulses in order to be punished, and of those who, by their chronic defiance, provoke retaliation. With adolescents, the need for punishment plays a part in their acting-out behavior, but it is questionable whether it is usually a dominant factor. A significant difference should be taken into account. The character formation of the adolescent is not structuralized but is still fluid. As a result, he acts out his defiance of his conscience in order to have a sense of freedom from it. His goal is not chiefly to gain punishment. Frightened by his freedom, however, he abandons his defiance and submits to his conscience. The conscience then behaves as parents behave when they punish a child for an act committed in their absence. Once the conscience is back in control, external punishment is sought or self-punishment is administered.

Parents as Symbols of the Conscience

As was pointed out earlier, the rebellion against the infantile conscience does not remain internal. The pattern of the conscience was determined by the parent-figures of infancy. This close relationship between internal and external forces makes possible a point of focus for the revolt. Parents may serve as a symbol of the conscience. As a result of the symbolization, part of the struggle can be externalized. The adolescent rebels against the parents and parent-surrogates not only because parents are restrictive but also because they are symbols of the infantile conscience from which the child must be partially free in order to reach maturity.

The adolescent's behavior toward his parents is as confused as it is toward his own conscience. At times he resents his parents' authority and flaunts his contempt for their beliefs and their pattern of living. At other times he seeks their controls, demands restrictions, and slavishly follows the family mores. He often violates those requirements that will bring punishment upon himself. The logical restrictions, which in themselves may not be too important in his daily living, are used for another purpose. He uses them as an excuse for rebellion, in trying to free himself of chains that are invisible but can be symbolized by the parent. At the same time, he values the restrictions since they assure him that external restraint against unfettered freedom exists and that punishment will follow if he oversteps the rules.

The value in violation of justifiable familial restrictions and in the resultant punishment was clearly shown in the following incident. George was 15 years old. His general pattern of behavior was characterized by constructive conformity both to the demands of his family and to those of his environment. The parents had only one major complaint. The trouble focused on the use of the family car. George was allowed to use the car at any time it was not needed by his mother. Frequently she would allow him to have it when she was aware that she would need it later in the day. Although ordinarily he was very reliable, on occasion he failed to return it on time. The parents finally punished him by refusing him the use of the car on the subsequent day, but he did not "learn his lesson," and failed again to return the car promptly. When his mother decided to handle the situation by completing her errands first and allowing him to have the car afterwards for an unrestricted period, a new source of irritation developed. Before he would use the car he insisted that his mother set a time for his return. He was able to verbalize a feeling of uneasiness and dissatisfaction if he drove off without a limit put on the time that he could be gone.

Alice, who was 14, created a somewhat similar situation. She was also very reliable. Her mother had overheard her, on several occasions, complain to her girl friends that her mother was too strict—that she made Alice come home from parties at a certain hour rather than allowing her to remain until the parties broke up.

The mother decided that she herself undoubtedly had been unreasonable. One night, as Alice was leaving for a party, she asked what time she was to return. The mother suggested that they not set a definite time but that Alice use her own judgment. Alice immediately rejected her mother's liberality. She asked her mother to state a definite time, explaining that even though she fussed at this restriction, actually she would feel uneasy if it were not imposed. She could not decide with any conviction what was the right time to leave. She preferred that her mother carry the burden. Alice also admitted that the restriction set by her mother served a further purpose. The time that her mother set usually coincided with her own wishes. If she should tell her friends that she wanted to go home they might criticize her. If she said that she had to go home because her mother was restrictive, she could save face with her friends by blaming her mother and at the same time could carry out her own wishes. She also confessed that sometimes when no restrictions had been imposed she pretended they had been —if her group wanted to do something that she did not wish to do. She would say her mother would not let her, even though this placed her mother in an unpleasant light. By this subterfuge, Alice consciously avoided the responsibility for failure to follow the group, transforming her distaste for an activity into a prohibition by her mother.

Although, in this instance, the subterfuge was used consciously, the same mechanism can be used unconsciously. When the adolescent wishes both to obey and to defy the conscience, he often externalizes the conscience by using the parent as its symbol. Such symbolic use of the parent may lead to a naïve interpretation of an adolescent's report of parental controls. He may say that a certain act would be prohibited by the parents when actually they have no objection. Superficially, such statements may be a result of simple misunderstanding of the parents' attitude, and sometimes may not be more complicated. In other instances, however, the adolescent is actually revealing the role of his own censor. He does not feel comfortable in carrying out the impulse behind the act and projects the disapproval onto the parent. Reassurance that the parent does not disapprove may lead to the conviction on the part of the adolescent that the act is proper and therefore should be accepted. On the other hand, unless he understands his own role in the prohibition, reassurance may only add to his anxiety and confusion.

The complex interaction of the role of the conscience, the role of the parent per se, and the role of the parent as a projection of the conscience, as well as the satisfaction that lies in the revolt against both the parent and the conscience, were illustrated by Jean's reaction to a rather simple situation. Jean's parents were well aware that high school girls and boys smoked. In discussion with her, the parents expressed their opinion that there was no convincing proof that smoking was either injurious or desirable for young people, but that, probably, it was wise to delay smoking as long as possible. They added that she very shortly would find herself with friends who smoked and they suggested that she might like to try it at home. They told her there was no need to hide the fact that she was smoking but that she might join them in an after-dinner cigarette. She did not accept the invitation, but eventually her parents became aware that she was smoking in her room. One evening after dinner her father passed her a cigarette, suggesting that since she was already smoking she might as well smoke with them. Jean blushed and very self-consciously took a cigarette and smoked it briefly. It took several days before she could smoke relaxedly in front of her parents. Her self-consciousness was not due to lack of skill; she no longer appeared an amateur once she was comfortable with her parents. She herself later described her feelings. She explained that she felt that she was doing something wrong in smoking in front of her parents even though her parents had not forbidden it. When she smoked prior to their knowledge she had a gratifying feeling of doing something wrong. When she no longer had to keep smoking a secret from her parents she noticed the enjoyment in smoking was much less. The simple episode evidently involved an unconscious prohibition against smoking, a prohibition which she identified with her parents and against which she secretly revolted.

Influence of the Peer Group

During the period of early adolescence, when the rebellion against the infantile superego seems to threaten all previously accepted standards of behavior, the modification of the superego by the mores of the peer group becomes apparent. The peer group, during latency, has not completely destroyed the earlier superego. It has only introduced certain modifications. Many parental standards are valued by the group as they are by the family structure. Stealing, for example, is prohibited by the family. Although a group frequently experiments with pilfering, in most instances it learns that stealing not only brings punishment from others as well as the parents, but jeopardizes the possessions of the group itself. Pressure against stealing comes from the group and ultimately results in a strengthening of the unconscious restraining force within the individual. The average social group, wishing to be accepted in the social structure, does not abandon the more important prohibitions that parents imposed earlier upon each individual. The acceptance by the child of this group-formulated pattern of behavior gives the child a sense of security in his world of classmates and friends.

Security with peers becomes extremely significant at adolescence. The panic resulting from unresolved conflicts at this age is handled in part by the individual's seeking a haven in the security his peer group offers. Frightened by his own impulses, and by the hazards of seemingly necessary complete repression, or alternatively, by the free expression of these impulses, he turns to the peer group for support and for answers to his questions. In the peer group he can discuss his mixed feelings and find solace in the identical suffering of others. He can formulate tentative answers to his perplexities, exposing them to the check of the equally tentative formulations of his peers. Most important, he can participate in the formulation of restrictions upon his behavior, which will assure him of protection from a chaotic expression of desires without the apparent dangers inherent in depending on the restrictions outlined by the parents.

Adolescent groups frequently have seemingly ridiculous rules of conduct as a part of the mores of their own world. There was, for example, a period in which an adolescent girl would have preferred walking down the street in a bathrobe to appearing with a cardigan sweater worn with the buttons in front. The group had decreed that to be "proper" a cardigan should be buttoned in back. The normal adolescent is a slave to the rules and fashions of the group.

THE FATE OF THE CONSCIENCE

The absurdities of the group-imposed restrictions frequently provoke expressions of ridicule or censorship from the adult world. The value of the group control is not always properly estimated. The group not only determines how a cardigan should be worn, but, more important, it tempers the effect of the rebellion against the infantile conscience. As a result of the mutual soul-searching that the individuals in the group experience, standards of the group concerning more basic concepts of social living take shape. Attitudes toward questions of morality, ethics, and social customs take form. The standards are rigidly held to by the individuals in the group and gradually become a part of the "conscience" of each member. The character of the group attitudes is influenced to a large degree by the past experiences of its members. If the past experiences have been generally satisfactory, the resulting group attitudes will not be strikingly different from parental standards. Some variations, of course, will occur. These variations often become known as "social progress" twenty years later. The group structure, however, has served in the meantime as a relative island of security in a tumultuous world. It has protected the individual from becoming lost in the tortuous paths and possibly the blind alleys of the psychological maze of adolescence.

VIII. Treatment through Supportive Measures

IT IS NOT SURPRISING that adults find adolescents challenging and irritating, baffling and obvious, charming and crude, stimulating and dull, frustrating and gratifying. The normal adolescent has at one time or another any or all of these contradictory characteristics. He will retain them until he either gives up the struggle and returns to a pre-adolescent psychological structure, or masters the conflicts and finds a satisfactory, adult resolution of them. The function of those working with and interested in adolescents is to strengthen the forces leading to the latter solution and to lessen the impact of the opposing forces. There are numerous detailed ways in which such help may be given.

The adolescent needs to experiment with his intensified drive toward maturation. He cannot be protected from all frustrations and dangers that lie in exploration. Only by trying his strength can he test his adequacy. Only by experiencing some of the frustrations and hazards of maturation can he learn to deal with the reality world as separate from his fantasies. Only by experiencing the satisfactions of independent activities can he resist the lure of permanent childhood.

On the other hand, he is apt to expose himself impulsively or through lack of perspective to situations that lie beyond his capacity. Thus, he needs, along with oportunities to be independent, guidance in undertaking new experiences. He will benefit from a framework that will limit his sphere of activity to challenging but achievable and acceptable goals. One of the most difficult problems of the adults who are responsible for adolescents is to establish a rapport with the young person which makes it possible for him to have the freedom he needs, yet assures his acceptance of guidance and restrictions. Without this rapport, wisely motivated supervision by an adult leads only to defiance and counter-behavior on the part of the adolescent.

Adolescent's Use of a Relationship

The adolescent profits not only from an opportunity to try out his newly found strength in new areas of independence; he is also helped by the assurance of support when he becomes baffled, ineffective, or frightened. He needs, therefore, people upon whom he can be dependent if he becomes frightened, but who will not demand continued dependency when he feels more assured and adequate in an independent role.

As he turns to someone to meet his dependency needs, he may develop a "crush." This situation often appears quite alarming to the adult observing it. Often the most obvious aspect of the attachment is its sexual implication. The sexual drive of the adolescent becomes directed toward one particular person, a person who in reality should not be the focus of sexual love. If the adolescent has turned to a person of the opposite sex, the situation often seems more amusing than serious to observers unless it reaches pathological intensity. If the love object is a person of the same sex, the relationship may be interpreted as homosexual and usually is seriously frowned upon. In most instances, however, the sexual component of the relationship is secondary in importance. The primary significance is related to the dependency needs of the adolescent, which he is seeking to gratify. Because adolescence is a period of awakening sexual feelings, which are not goal directed at the time, the desire for dependency gratification becomes erotized; the dependency and sexual needs are fused. Most commonly, the sexual interest in the love object lessens in intensity as the dependency needs are adequately met. An adolescent does not become involved in a "crush" unless he has a strong need for some gratification that he believes this other person can meet.

The adolescent's urge to establish a relationship with a person who offers some dependency gratification may result in a relationship that has many values. The young person is seeking someone by whom he will feel completely accepted; he wishes to find protection from the forces of a frightening reality; he wants help in dealing with the internal drives that are so difficult for him to understand and to master; he wants a guardian who will protect him much as parents did in the past. Furthermore, he is confused about the type of person he wants to be. As indicated in an earlier chapter, the definitive lines of his ego-ideal are fuzzy. Having found a person he loves and by whom he wishes to be loved, he utilizes the relationship as a small child utilizes his relationship with his parents. He attempts to structuralize the type of person he wants to be in accordance with his concept of what the loved person is and wishes of him.

If the adolescent has found gratification in a relationship with a person of the same sex, he often imitates the love object's manner of dress, his mode of speech, and his habits of living. This manifest behavior is the outward sign of a deeper mimicry that is coloring his thoughts and emotional patterns. If the individual to whom he has responded is of the opposite sex, the young person strives to behave in accordance with any indication he has of what that person expects of him. He will often show slavish, almost hypnotic devotion to the person's wishes. The adolescent's love object may be not only a person who can serve as a protective parent-surrogate but also may be someone who offers direction for him as he seeks to become the individual he wishes to be. Dissatisfied with his own image of himself, he seeks another image he can emulate. In this way he hopes to gain more self-acceptance as well as greater acceptance by the external world.

Frequently, in his devotion to the love object, the individual's behavior is colored by a great deal of hostility. The striking characteristic of this hostility is its artificial nature. If the hostility were genuine it would be difficult to understand why the object of it is sought after. As the hostility is acted out, it can be seen that it serves several roles; its significance varies from individual to individual. The hostility may be primarily seductive, as if it were a more acceptable way to attract the attention of the other person than a more obvious form of seduction. Sometimes it seems to be motivated by a desire to provoke punishment from a loved person, permitting an erotization of the suffering the punishment would bring. Undoubtedly the hostility is often an exaggerated manifestation of the normal ambivalence of the period; it then may express the adolescent's feeling that the demands that are being imposed upon him are beyond his capacity to fulfil. His anger is a means of denying both his fear of rejection and the implications of his own inadequacy. It should also be borne in mind that frequently the intensity of the adolescent's feeling for an older person is frightening to the young person so that, much as he needs it, he wishes to deny its existence. His hostility then is an attempt to hide the fear that the relationship creates and to deny the intensity of its meaning. In addition, if he has great dependency needs, the relationship does not and cannot adequately meet his demands. He has been led to expect gratification and, when he feels it has been withheld from him, he responds with anger at the person who has failed him. As has been mentioned earlier, the hostility, whatever its roots, frequently has an unreal quality, as if the adolescent were being pressed into a role that he does not take too seriously himself.

If handled wisely, a "crush" can be a valuable experience for an emotionally needful adolescent. Unfortunately, the recipient of the adolescent's affection often either is frightened by the relationship or seeks to meet his own neurotic needs through it. The adult in such instances fails to give support that is needed in a form that will be helpful.

If the adult is frightened by the adolescent's attachment, he may attempt to break off the relationship abruptly, either by ignoring the adolescent, by ridiculing him, or by criticizing him sharply. Such rebuffs can have serious immediate repercussions. The adolescent feels deserted by someone he loves and by whom he believed himself loved. An experience of this nature also is a warning against forming similar relationships. He then may withdraw from meaningful contacts at a time when he is unable to master his own problems, and be forced to struggle alone with problems for which he has inadequate knowledge or inadequate experience. As a result, he may reach an unwise solution which might have been avoided had the adult to whom he had turned offered him wise guidance and constructive support.

When the adult is gratifying a neurotic need of his own in the relationship, the immediate repercussions may be less dramatic and less apparent than when the adult pushes the adolescent away. The ultimate damage, however, may be even more severe. He may meet the immediate needs of the adolescent but in doing so bind him to the adult's own neurosis. If the adult is expressing his own homosexual interests in the relationship, he gratifies the adolescent's dependency needs but does not leave him free to escape from the relationship. The erotization of the relationship may reach such an intensity that the adolescent becomes fixated to a homosexual orientation or, on the other hand, becomes frightened by the intensity of his homosexual feelings and runs away from the adult in homosexual panic. As a result of this experience he may avoid any further close relationships, fearing that he will expose himself to the same danger. He may also misinterpret his own sexual impulses and brand himself a homosexual.

Role of the Adult in a Relationship

If the adult, instead of rejecting the relationship or meeting his own neurotic needs through it, is able to maintain a role that offers gratification of the adolescent's dependency needs, he can do much toward strengthening the young person's ego capacity to deal with his internal conflicts and his external reality. The adult must also be able to recognize evidence of growing independence in the individual and to foster it. The adolescent should not feel that he will lose the gratification he has found in the relationship if he gradually establishes himself as a more independent person. The adult should serve the dual function of a wise parent: he should accept dependency and encourage maturation.

The value that can derive to the adolescent from an intense relationship—if the recipient of the young person's love handles it wisely—seems to be validated by clinical observation. The author, in the role of consultant at a camp for adolescent girls, has had an opportunity to see such relationships in action. At the beginning of the camp period the counselors, who on the whole are rather young but usually stable persons, are given a theoretical orientation to the meaning of "crushes."

When one of the campers becomes strongly attached to a counselor, careful supervision is given to her in her work with the girl. If the counselor cannot handle the relationship, immediate steps are taken to shift the focus of the camper's attention to another counselor more able to handle such problems. The relationship with the first can usually be transferred to the second person. During this early period, it is not the contact with a particular person which is of importance to the girl but rather the finding of someone to fill a void in her emotional life. As the relationship develops between the girl and the counselor, no attempt is made to divert the girl from her love attachment, if the adult is able to handle it wisely. Other adults on the staff are encouraged to be casual and friendly in their contacts with the girl. When she leaves camp, she is encouraged, if she wishes, to maintain contact with the counselor through correspondence.

The strong attachment to the counselor seems actually to stimulate the girl to seek other positive relationships with adults and does not, as might be expected, lead her to isolate herself from further contacts. It is not unusual for the social agency that sends the girl to camp to report that the girl has been unable to form a meaningful relationship with the social worker. After a close living experience in which she forms a strong tie to the counselor, the girl, on her return to her old environment and her former social worker, frequently is much more responsive to the social worker. Obviously, the girl's ability to use both relationships is facilitated if the social worker does not feel competitive with the counselor, but values the counselor's experience with the girl and utilizes the knowledge the counselor has gained to modify her own approach.

This transfer of feelings from the counselor to the worker is often aided when the counselor can point out to the girl that she might obtain some of the help she desires through the social worker. Opportunities for making this suggestion often occur in the correspondence following camp. If a girl writes to her counselor expressing concern over her school or home situation, the counselor, in replying, may express sympathy and her hope that it can be corrected, adding that since she is not close enough to the situation to make any recommendations, the social worker is the person best equipped to help the girl. She therefore urges her to talk over the problem frankly with the worker. The counselor neither rejects the girl nor competes with the social worker in the relationship. She tries to help the girl to value both relationships.

The close relationship of a girl to a counselor at camp and during the post-camp period may have disastrous results if it has not been handled wisely. Occasionally, in spite of close surveillance, the counselor rebuffs the girl or utilizes the relationship to meet her own neurotic needs. The termination of the camp period then can be extremely traumatic for the girl. Also, the after-effects of the relationship may be catastrophic if the social worker cannot accept the counselor's role and function.

In one situation the social worker had been attempting for some time to establish a relationship with a very withdrawn, hostile girl, but had been completely unsuccessful. At camp, the girl at first was resistant to any interest shown by the counselors, but finally attached herself to a mature, stable counselor. The counselor handled the relationship skilfully, and recognized the necessity of gradually transferring the relationship to the social worker at home. For reasons that appeared theoretically sound, the psychiatrist supervising the case recommended that the counselor withdraw on the girl's return home, ignoring her letters and telephone calls, in order to leave the field free for the social worker. The girl became extremely upset and panicky. Her relationship with the worker, which had formerly been neutral, now became overtly hostile. It was apparent from her letters to the counselor that she felt trapped in her conflicts, with no one to turn to; she was deserted by the one person who had meaning to her. The psychiatric diagnosis was "homosexual panic." It seems more likely that the panic was the result of the desertion.

It is true that, in this instance, the intense relationship with the counselor proved ultimately to be unfortunate. Other experiences, however, with girls of a similar type, when they have been permitted to retain such a relationship, have brought beneficial results. It seems likely that the relationship with the counselor in this particular case was disastrous because its termination was not wisely handled, rather than because of truly unhealthy elements in it.

Since the adolescent is attempting, through his relationship with an older person, to find a more satisfactory ego-ideal for himself, further complications exist in efforts to utilize the relationship as a therapeutic agent. Many people assume that because the adolescent characteristically is rebellious against adults, he will not accept a relationship with an older person unless the adult denies his own maturity. The adult then strives to present himself as an adolescent, implying that he can completely identify with the younger person because they are both struggling with exactly the same problems.

The confusion that may result for the adolescent when the adult presents himself in this fashion was clearly stated by an adolescent girl who was referred for psychiatric treatment because of acute anxiety. She had formed a very close relationship with a teacher. At first she seemed to gain considerable gratification from this relationship and then, following a prolonged conversation with her, she developed severe anxiety. Preliminary evaluation of the situation suggested that the conversation had precipitated an acute homosexual panic. Exploration proved fruitless, however, as long as it was based upon this assumption. As treatment progressed the precipitating factor became clear. In her conversation with the teacher, the girl had revealed a feeling of anger toward her mother, although actually she was very attached to her mother. She was attempting to repress these positive feelings in order to free herself of the guilt aroused by her hostile feelings. The positive feelings were too real and her sense of guilt had become overwhelming. She was aware that the teacher frequently visited her own mother. She had thought the teacher's daughter-mother relationship was a pleasant one, and had sought out the teacher in the hope that through talking over the problem with her she would understand more about her own feelings. Instead, when she presented the problem to the teacher, the older woman expressed extremely hostile feelings toward her own mother, unburdening herself to the young girl. The teacher wept as she confessed her guilt about her conflictual relationship with her mother whom she both loved and hated.

To the therapist, the girl recalled that at that moment she herself became intensely anxious. The revelation by the older woman meant to her that the problem of ambivalent feelings toward one's mother was insoluble. She finally said, "When will adults realize that when a person of my age turns to them for help, she does so because she feels that the older person must have found some answer we cannot find? If we want to talk to others who are as confused as we are, we can go to people of our own age. We do not want to be told by older people that we have to feel as they do or that we have to accept their solutions. We do want to know that older people have found an answer that gives some peace to them even though we finally may find a different one. Why can't older people tell us what they think, or what solutions other people have found? We want to know that there are answers but we want to be free to choose the one that meets our needs the most."

The adolescent's use of the adult as an ego-ideal places a real responsibility upon the older person. Because of the intensity of the emotional tie that the adolescent feels toward this love object, he will not be capable of making a wise choice as he strives to imitate the latter's behavior. He may accept uncritically both the desirable and the undesirable elements of the love object's behavior. If the love object is a person who has made a relatively constructive adaptation as an adult, he will be a constructive force in the adaptation of the adolescent. If he has made an unfortunate adjustment, he will be an equally destructive force.

People who meet life with the assumption that they know the only correct answer to any problem should never work with adolescents. Such rigidity necessitates rebellion on the part of the adolescent in order to assure himself that he has freedom of choice. Similarly, people who have not found a workable philosophy and who are themselves in a state of confusion, are not capable of dealing with adolescents. The adult who will work most effectively with them is the individual who is relatively comfortable in his own adjustment but who is genuinely tolerant of other constructive patterns of adjustment.

It is important that adults realize the extreme sensitiveness of the adolescent. His state is comparable to that observed in an inflamed nerve. Slight stimulation may result in vigorous, undirected response. This sensitivity causes the adolescent to take seriously remarks that were intended as friendly teasing or a bit of humor. Parents and other adults will often comment in a derogatory way about the adolescent's appearance, his ability, or his behavior. Although it may be a casual remark referring to an incident of the moment, to the adolescent it is often a verification of his own suspicion that he is not attractive or adequate. A teasing approach to the adolescent is not wise unless the adolescent is quite confident that he is basically accepted by the person who does the teasing. Such confidence does not result from verbal reassurance but comes only from the experience of feeling genuinely accepted. The genuineness is demonstrated by a sympathetic but casual tolerance shown by the adult toward the irritability, moodiness, unrealistic ambitions, and unrealistic sense of failure revealed by the adolescent. Teasing always carries some implication of hostility, rejection, or belittling, and thus is always a questionable tool.

Ponderous, pontifical seriousness is not the only alternative to teasing. A "light touch" is not necessarily a teasing one. Frequently the adolescent is reassured if the adult reveals a sense of humor about the problems that exist, particularly if the adult is not laughing at the adolescent but is helping him to see the humorous aspects of a situation. The very fact that the adult is not overwhelmed by the problems presented reassures the young person. A too consistently solemn approach may be frightening by its implication that the multiple difficulties of life are all uniformly serious and weighty. The adolescent too often knows that the realities are not as serious as the older person implies by his solemnity. The obvious lack of perspective on the part of the older person can invalidate his conclusions.

Freedom and Limits

The adolescent's need to revolt and his anxiety about the implications of the revolt present perhaps the most difficult situations for the adult to handle wisely. Freedom extending beyond the individual's knowledge and ability to deal with it leads to license or to panic. The young person is not prepared to deal with the intensity of internal drives and the pressure of external demands without assistance. His experiences with freedom should be within a framework of wisely determined limits. What these limits should be differ from individual to individual and from one situation to another. They should be flexible—broadened as the individual shows the capacity to handle a problem and narrowed when the capacity narrows. Rules established by adults for the adolescent should be designed to strengthen his impulse toward mature behavior rather than to bind him to infancy. The rules give security to the adolescent, assuring him that outside agents will prevent him from carrying his revolt to the serious point of harm to himself or others.

Some persons who work with adolescents have a tendency, at present, to be too permissive, perhaps in a reaction to a former trend to handle all children too rigidly. As a result, high school students often are given too much responsibility for controlling their own behavior and making their own decisions. The Victorian concept of chaperonage was certainly crippling to the development of maturity. The complete absence of such control, however, leaves the young people at the mercy of impulses that they cannot handle. Theoretically, if the adolescent has an ideal relationship with parents or parent-surrogates, constructive control is maintained *in absentia*. Rarely in reality is the relationship with guiding adults so satisfactory.

Clinically, the effect of too great freedom is discernible in two diametrically opposing patterns of behavior. On the one hand, the individual may be so frightened by the responsibility placed upon him for self-control that he is paralyzed and unable to express his impulses in any form, desirable or otherwise. On the other hand, the individual may accept the freedom as tacit permission to act out his impulses whenever the pressure is sufficient to warrant such behavior; as a result he may drink excessively, be sexually promiscuous, keep hours that are poor from a hygienic standpoint, or fail to apply himself to his academic work. Although in some instances such behavior is the result of deep, underlying conflicts, frequently it may be simply an immediate expression of impulses that are not constructively goal-directed. They are being expressed in this form because of the absence of external control at a time when the internal mechanisms of control are inadequate.

Many parents have been oversold on the idea of freedom for the adolescent and should be helped to learn the value of sane restrictions. In many instances parents fail to impose wise restrictions because of the vicarious gratification they derive from the delinquency of their child. They justify the vicarious gratification by defending the modern attitude of permitting greater freedom for the adolescent.

It should not be assumed, however, that all parents are neurotically motivated. Often, a parent is intellectually convinced of the so-called modern methods and, against his own intuitive judgment, accepts the recommendation for greater freedom for young people. Not really understanding the implications of the recommendation, he may carry it beyond the limits that wisdom would dictate. Parents should be helped to understand adolescence rather than be given specific rules or prescribed ways of reacting. Social workers and others who understand the psychology of adolescence can give considerable help to the parents because they are less emotionally involved in the relationship. They should bear in mind that the average parent of the average adolescent is as confused as the adolescent is. It cannot be repeated too often that the parents of an adolescent should be carefully evaluated. They should not be condemned before they are tried.

While limits are important, it is equally important that the limits not prevent the adolescent from carrying through successfully a part of his revolt. The protective devices of childhood become shackles that must be thrown off if maturation is to occur. The revolt against these crippling fetters causes a sharp sense of guilt. If this guilt becomes too great, the revolt will be abandoned. The adolescent needs reassurance from others that his feeling of guilt may be unwarranted or too great. He should not be freed of all guilt. Guilt, if reasonable in intensity and the result of violation of healthy standards of behavior, is an important stimulus to integration. The young person frequently needs help in understanding the nature of his guilt in order to use it constructively rather than as a tool for chaining himself to his infantile patterns. Again, he needs help from a person who not only understands the value of the revolt but who personally has reached a level of maturity that permits him to deal with his own reality world with constructive, dynamic adaptation rather than with passive submission or destructive rebellion.

Value of Parental Support

An adolescent needs parents. He may be critical of his parents, but he still needs them. Often the criticism makes sense. Persons working with adolescents, who feel an empathy with them, are tempted to identify with them and reject the parents. Such identification often results in the adult's pressing the young person prematurely to escape emotionally, if not physically, from his parents. The pressure may result in one or a combination of several possible, unfortunate responses.

1. Perhaps the adolescent wishes to abandon the parents but fears to take the step. The parents have had too many positive values, in providing at least a modicum of security, to make the abandonment seem safe. Frightened by the stimulus from another person to reject the parents, the adolescent in acute anxiety reverts to greater dependency upon the parents in order to negate the temptation that seems fraught with danger.

2. Unable to carry through the revolt, either for practical or emotional reasons, the adolescent may deny his own inadequacies by projecting the blame upon the adult who encouraged the revolt. He then views him as a dangerous and undesirable person. Not he himself but his adviser is bad. This projection robs him of a valuable part of himself, leaving his child-self in command, with his drive for maturation displaced upon another who is evil. His adviser not only loses his value as a helper, but, in precipitating his own destruction, destroys part of the psychological structure of the adolescent.

3. Some unimportant episode may result in a young person's verbalizing a desire to rebel against his parents. The validity of the rebellion may appear obvious; the particular hazards inherent in the revolt, minor. Because of the apparent safety in the situation the rebellion is encouraged. The manifest situation, however, may be only the tip of a deeply submerged, large iceberg. Encouragement to become emancipated from the parents in minor details at a too early stage may mean encouragement to abandon all that the parents represent. Such abandonment is not safe except as new standards replace the old ones. The new standards may develop either through the relationship of the adolescent with a parent-surrogate who offers less paralyzing restrictions than the childhood ones or through the internal growth of the individual. Unless the adolescent has accepted, at least in part, a mature standard, a broad revolt against the parent may prove disastrous to the future pattern of behavior. Adolescents must free themselves

from their parents, but they need support in doing so. The emancipation will be most constructively handled if they are encouraged to gain their freedom by evolution rather than by revolution.

Group Experiences

The adolescent group exerts a stronger constructive influence on the individual than any one adult. The average adolescent can understand, accept, and assimilate the teachings of his own peers with greater facility than he can the teaching offered by individuals from a more psychologically alien world. His relationship to his peer group, confused as it may be, is less emotionally charged than his relationship with older people. The group can offer limitations, freedom, and standards in a more palatable form. It should be borne in mind that because of the adolescent's anxiety, he seeks the protection of conformity. His conformity most frequently is to the standards of his peer group; he rarely violates seriously the standards it imposes. If the peer group behavior can be guided to constructive patterns, most of the individuals in the group will develop the same patterns. Group psychology has a more direct and immediate effect on individual psychology at this age than in later life. Although group experience has value at any age, at adolescence, because of the responsiveness and the needs of the individual, it can be especially significant. A skilful group leader can often accomplish treatment aims that a therapist dealing with an individual cannot achieve.

Group experiences offer many learning opportunities for the adolescent. In establishing a satisfactory role for himself among his own age group, he is laying the foundation for his future role in the adult social world. His ultimate adult fulfilment, after all, will not be experienced in the social world of his parents, but rather in one that he and his peers will construct. Through his participation in sports, he experiences the satisfaction of gaining recognition from his friends. When sports involve team play, he learns of the individual satisfaction that can be gained through being a part of a social structure, a structure which not only is greater than he, but which cannot exist without his individual contribution. He experiences the satisfaction obtained through reaching a goal by mutual co-operation. How much happier human relationships would be if the patterns inherent in sportsmanship could be carried over into all aspects of living!

The corruption of college sports by bribery and organized gambling has tragic effects not only on the individuals involved, but also on all college students. One of the most important contributions that can be made to healthy psychological growth—the fostering of real sportsmanship—is threatened by such corruptive influences. Young persons suffer when adults provide poor standards of behavior for them. More disastrous, however, are the repercussions that have led to discrediting of the value of college sports. To deprive the young person of a living experience that involves honest constructive participation, either as a player or as a loyal observer, in teamwork would be most unfortunate. College could teach that the world is flat and no serious permanent damage would be done to the future generation. But if it teaches, by example, that the end justifies the means, the harm to society will be extensive. Those who advocate abolishing college competitive games because of an occasional unfortunate incident should ask themselves whether it is wise to burn a house down because the roof leaks.

Group experiences should not be limited to those in which the participants are of the same sex. Group activities in which boys and girls share have special values. In education, the wisdom of segregating the sexes is being questioned. In the past, many schools, especially those providing living facilities, extended the principle of segregation to include most of the social life. Currently, many are attempting to evolve a program in which the boys and girls are separated during classroom hours but are brought together for their social life. An argument frequently offered for segregated education is that the stimulation caused by the presence of the opposite sex adds to the young people's confusion about their heterosexual adjustment and affects their academic work. It is argued that, if the stimulation is not present, the adolescent's energy will be available for academic achievement. It is questionable whether this assumption is valid. The sexual problems of the adolescent are only secondarily caused by the presence of a person of the opposite sex. The root of the confusion lies in the effect of the impact of sexual maturation. That the problem is not avoided by segregation is indicated both by the greater frequency of homosexual acting out in schools where there is consistent segregation of the sexes, and also by the fact that the boys and girls in schools where the sexes are kept separate are as much if not more preoccupied with sexual fantasies as are the young people in situations where the sexes intermingle in everyday living.

Another aspect of the question should be appraised carefully. What should be the actual goals in teaching the adolescent? It is certainly true that many adolescents can be helped to direct their energy into academic achievement rather than into solving their sexual problems. Academic achievement can be an escape from the overwhelming typical conflicts of the age. Although segregation may be justified on the ground that an academic drive can be a sublimation of more basic drives that cannot be directly expressed, it is debatable whether the average adolescent is capable of complete, constructive sublimation. He is more apt to use an all-encompassing academic preoccupation as a means of avoiding and denying the pressing problems he faces. Adolescents can do well in their academic work without being disturbed individuals; that they are doing well at school is not, however, conclusive evidence that they are not emotionally disturbed.

Education is supposedly training for life. Although a knowledge of chemistry and Latin is undoubtedly an aid in reaching goals of adulthood, it is certainly questionable whether knowing Latin and chemistry is as important as knowing how to live in a bisexual, adult world. Adulthood is not reached until the individual resolves some of his adolescent problems. Academic learning at the high school level may be of secondary importance. A good academic experience is desirable if it is obtained without sacrificing the more basic process of maturation. Segregation in the high school years creates an artificial situation at a time when it is most crucial for the young person to learn to live with people of the opposite sex.

Schools that follow the principle of segregation, but attempt to bring the sexes together in social activities, emphasize only one aspect of heterosexual relationships. Boys and girls need to work, as well as to play, together. The problems of living in a bisexual world are not solely social or sexual. The problem of finding an ultimate place in the adult world, in which the man's and the woman's roles are different but complementary, must also be solved. It is likely that the more experiences are shared, the more easily this goal can be attained. Sharing an algebra problem or an unpleasant teacher, reacting differently to a poem or to a school crisis, teach more about shared living than can be learned on the dance floor. Without question, when a boy and girl share day-to-day activities, each is exposed to sexual stimulation by the other. Such stimulation is not something foreign to our culture or potentially destructive. It is a type of stimulation that the individual must learn to handle constructively. Such mastery may in the long run be easier to achieve if it is learned through actual life experiences instead of through fantasy in a vacuum, or only through recreational activities.

Under certain circumstances, segregation of the sexes is desirable. Occasionally a young adolescent is so overwhelmed by the many facets of his difficulties that he cannot deal with all of them at once. He then requires an environment where the number of problems that he faces is somewhat arbitrarily limited. Sometimes, because of deep, underlying disturbances, his response to the opposite sex is distorted, being utilized to express impulses that primarily are not sexually directed. The presence of the opposite sex then is so frightening that the individual feels paralyzed in all his activities, and, if removed from the disturbing influence, he can more readily use his inherent capacities. When segregation in education or in social life seems desirable, such a program usually should be considered as transitional, and should be accompanied by appropriate individual treatment. The aim of treatment should be to help the individual deal with the underlying problems that have necessitated the protective environment. As soon as possible he should enter the world in which he will spend his adult life—a world that is bisexual.

The adolescent is striving to orient himself to a new world. Often he can be helped most successfully to gain orientation by guidance and support as he acquires actual experience in that world. His natural impulses will provide the incentive for growth. Distortions in that growth frequently can be minimized if the positive aspects of his own psychological potentialities and the constructive resources of his environment are utilized in treatment plans that will provide an optimum milieu for development.

IX. Psychiatric Treatment of the Adolescent

THE INITIAL CONTACT with adolescents who either are seeking help with their emotional problems on their own initiative or are sent by parents to obtain help often suggests that insight-focused psychotherapy would be the therapy of choice. Particularly is this true when the young person himself is aware of his difficulties and wishes to understand them. It is not unusual to have material spontaneously offered in the initial interview which appears to give the broad outlines of the fundamental problems. The patient expresses alarm about his response to the parent of the opposite sex and his fear and resentment of the parent of the same sex. He discusses his sense of social inadequacy and recognizes its origin in his inability to compete with his parents. He may also speak of his preoccupation with bodily functions, his fantasies of smearing, and his erotized desire to suck at the breast like an infant. When material that the adult characteristically disguises, represses, and denies, is revealed so readily, the temptation is to give further insight into the underlying motivations and drives through interpretative therapy.

There is one obvious fallacy in this treatment plan. The initial interview has revealed that the individual has a great deal of awareness of the meaning of his feelings, but does not know what to do with the insight he has. With the adolescent who can verbalize so directly his underlying disturbances, and yet who appears so helpless in dealing with them, a treatment technique differing from that used either in child or in adult therapy seems indicated.

In child therapy, if a small boy does not have an awareness of his attachment to his mother, it may be necessary—if treatment is to be successful—that he understand the nature of the tie and the unwise defenses he has mobilized against its implications. This is only the first step in child therapy. Once the child recognizes his problem, the educational aspect begins. The child is helped by the therapist to recognize the reality that he cannot replace his father. In treatment he is helped to abandon an unattainable goal and his destructive defenses and is encouraged to build up constructively adaptive defenses.[1] In a parallel situation in adolescence, the boy may recognize the nature of his conflict about his mother as well as the basis for his fear and hostility toward his father. At the same time he knows the reality situation—that he cannot replace his rival. He does not need the type of educational approach utilized in child therapy.

In adult therapy, the presenting problem by the patient is characteristically the external manifestation of the defenses mobilized against an unacceptable impulse. Consciously the patient is unaware of such impulses. His defenses are crippling because they are activated in response to situations that are falsely identified with the original, related situation that necessitated the formation of the defensive structure. Thus, the man who cannot marry may be unable to marry because every woman symbolizes his mother. He must protect himself against his incestuous impulses. He can do so only by isolating himself from all women. Insight of therapeutic value, therefore, is that which helps him not only to recognize the nature of his original tie to his mother and his transference of that feeling to all women, but which also helps him to distinguish other women from his mother. Psychoanalysis of adults does not free the individual to gratify his incestuous impulses but frees him from the crippling effect of those defenses that served a useful purpose in controlling the infantile incestuous impulses impinging upon other areas of his emotional life. With this liberation, his love can turn to an ego-accepted love object.

An adolescent boy who is conscious of his tie to his mother is

[1] See Berta Bornstein, "On Latency," *The Psychoanalytic Study of the Child*, Vol. VI, International Universities Press, New York, 1951, 279-285.

disturbed primarily not because of the symbolic meaning of other sexual relationships but because all his libidinal energy is bound to the incestuous conflict. Interpretation, then, is only a repetition of what he already knows. Although it is true that usually other women are identified with the mother and the prohibition against incest is inhibiting the establishment of heterosexual relationships, this, in early adolescence, is not so significant as is the intensity of the emotional investment he has made in his relationship to his mother. The individual is developing defenses but the defenses are not as yet sufficiently organized to result in consistently effective displacement.

In those cases where the adolescent reveals very directly the nature of his conflict, careful scrutiny frequently suggests that the very rawness of the problem constitutes a potential danger for intensive interpretative therapy. Regardless of how crippling defenses may be to the individual, the very fact that the individual has established certain defenses is a sign of ego strength. The transparency of the problems that young adolescents often verbalize is evidence of a temporary weakness in the individual's ego structure. The boy who evinces real anxiety as he reveals his awareness of his own sexual response to his mother may be revealing the return to consciousness of his earlier feeling toward her. The fact that this feeling has broken through in an undisguised form suggests that the ego has been overwhelmed and is unable to defend itself from the impact of formerly unconscious impulses. Forcing the individual to face more completely the significance of his relationship with his mother may result in an increased burden to and resultant greater deterioration of the ego. Therapy may then be interpreted by the patient as permission to indulge himself in the incestuous fantasy. He can avoid the task of constructively sublimating his libidinal drive. Relieved of guilt, he can escape the restrictions of healthy defenses and abandon his struggle for sexual maturation. The attempt at treatment has only strengthened the urge to remain emotionally bound to the mother.

In contrast to the adolescent who verbalizes readily his underlying problems, the therapist is often confronted with an adolescent who is completely unable to verbalize his difficulties. In some instances he is unable to verbalize them because he is protecting himself. By complete repression of any conscious awareness of their nature, he avoids the discomfort that awareness would cause. In other instances he is consciously withholding information. Whether he fails to verbalize his feelings for conscious or unconscious reasons he has, as far as his own psychological economy is concerned, no therapeutic goal. He wishes to have the external world made comfortable for him. He wants his parents, not himself, to be different. Because of the battering the ego is experiencing, a protective wall has been constructed. The individual is saying, in effect, that he cannot by internal mechanisms handle any greater pressure from the external world. He must be relieved from the external pressure before he can mobilize his internal forces constructively. He is functioning as might a company of soldiers which, attacked from all sides, takes shelter behind a barricade. Its first step in planning is to protect itself from multiple attacks. It will re-form into an efficiently performing unit only as it gains some protection by means of the barricade. If the barricade is efficient and discipline has not disintegrated as a result of the attack, the unit can be re-formed into an attacking organization. If, however, before this occurs the barricades are destroyed by the attacking forces, the company is routed. If, in therapy, the protective devices of the individual are broken down before the individual has a chance to organize more effective techniques, he will be overwhelmed.

When psychiatric treatment is indicated for the adolescent, the treatment of choice appears to be one that considerably modifies both child psychoanalysis and the more classical form of adult psychoanalysis. The individual needs, first of all, to be protected from the external situations that excessively stimulate his internal drives. For example, in the case of the boy who is struggling with his tie to his mother, he needs to be protected from any seductive behavior on her part. In addition, he needs help in redirecting his libidinal drive toward less anxiety-stimulating love objects. He needs an opportunity to sublimate his unacceptable primitive drives into socially acceptable, psychologically constructive paths. Insight therapy should be utilized only when such redirection is impossible. Three illustrative cases follow.

Ruth

A case in which the individual was consciously aware of the basic problem that was creating the difficulty, and in which the nature of treatment was clear, is illustrated in the study and treatment of Ruth. She was an extremely intelligent girl of 16, who came to a psychiatrist for treatment because of a rather common symptom in the adolescent girl, painful menstruation. Her menstrual cramps were extremely severe; every month she was incapacitated for two or three days. She stated quite frankly when she came to the initial interview that she was certain that her menstrual cramps related to her general tension. She knew a little about psychiatric treatment since an uncle had been psychoanalyzed. She did not wish to be "analyzed"; she only wanted her tension relieved. She stated very definitely that she was frightened by the things that her uncle had found out about himself. The uncle had not been particularly exhibitionistic about his treatment. She obviously had pressed him to discuss it in order to determine its nature.

In spite of her fear of deeper therapy, her review of her life situation was suprisingly frank. Her father was a teacher of philosophy, a very intelligent and verbal individual. From the time she was a small child he had chosen to discuss his thoughts with her rather than with her mother. As a result, as she grew older she shared his taste in reading, spending much of her free time reading philosophy. This she discussed with him. In contrast to her closeness to her father, she felt remote from her mother. She explained that her mother was stupid; her mother never read books of any importance and spent a great deal of her time in foolish social activities. Her one asset was that she was an excellent cook and housekeeper. These tasks were something she did not have to do since the father, as a result of inherited wealth, could have provided adequate domestic help. The mother, however, insisted upon being "the maid in the house," doing the cooking and housework. To Ruth, this was only further evidence of her mother's real inadequacy in the world that was open to human beings of intelligence. As far as contact with girls or boys of her own age was concerned, Ruth had only contempt for that part of her life. She did date. She did not really know why, because she was not particularly interested in the more frivolous side of life. She dated a boy who was quite obviously mentally inferior to her, but whom she described as physically attractive. He was also very kind and somewhat seductive with her. She rather regretfully acknowledged that she enjoyed the seduction, which remained well within conventional bounds. She felt no companionability with girls her own age because they were not interested in really important things. They were primarily interested in boys, parties, and doing "silly things." She repeatedly referred to the closed circle created by her father and herself. She described what she considered the unimportant part of her life as made up of episodes with her mother and her friends, episodes that only filled in the time. Her real living came in her close intellectual companionship with her father.

At the end of the first hour, having given the preceding material, Ruth, with a burst of frankness which obviously carried a great deal of emotional affect, stated that there was one thing about her relationship with her father that frightened her, which she had not wanted to tell. She had observed recently that when he showed her any type of affection, either physical or verbal, she experienced the same gratification she had when her boy friend showed similar affection. She felt there must be something very wrong about her which caused her to react in this way. She then defended herself by saying that after all her father was more attractive than any boy she had ever known and that furthermore they had this close intellectual companionship. She felt that she probably would never find a man who could give her in marriage the satisfaction that her father gave her in their day-by-day living. She laughingly commented that her father felt there was no boy good enough for her and that probably she shared his opinion.

Even in this initial interview certain aspects of the problem stood out. The girl's incestuous tie to her father was only faintly veiled by the intellectual interests that the two shared. The significance of the mother in this picture was not so clear as it became subsequently. Later interviews disclosed that the mother was not quite the stupid person the girl originally described. Although her reading was not in philosophy, her choice of literature was on the whole similar to the choice of most intelligent people who read for escape purposes rather than intellectual enrichment. She was more interested in people than in intellectual abstractions. She showed a great deal of acuity in her understanding of people. Her supposedly purposeless activities out of the home were really rather important ones. She was an intelligent, guiding person in the League of Women Voters and the Parent-Teacher Association. She was a thoughtful member of the board of an excellent organization. She enjoyed her work in the home, seeing it as a creative outlet. She had found a way of living which not only utilized her intelligence but which made possible a sublimation of her creativeness in the framework of a feminine role in our society.

As Ruth's treatment progressed, the dynamics of her problem became clear. She was attempting to preserve the relationship with her father through disguising its significance by an intellectual displacement. She protected herself against the implication of her mother's role in the family by denying any validity to her mother's function. Actually she felt extremely inadequate as she compared herself with her mother. Her mother had charm and warmth that resulted in gratifying relationships with many people, relationships the girl felt she could not experience because she was too inadequate with her own age group. Ruth had not abandoned her femininity. She had not identified with her father but strove rather to express her femininity through an intellectual seduction of her father. She felt that she could not succeed as a woman through the more usual expression of femininity. She felt uncomfortable with boys, not because they were stupid but because she felt she was unattractive as a girl. Her contempt for her own age group was a denial of her actual feeling of inadequacy. Her dreams revealed a great deal of jealousy of the girls who not only could talk about "silly things" with other girls but who could also seduce boys. She wanted to be a sexually successful woman, but felt she could not be. She chose the second best answer in being an intellectual woman. Since her only success with men had been with her father, she was devoting her life to cementing that relationship.

Treatment in this case began with an attempt to strengthen the girl's confidence in herself by recognizing the universality of her feeling of inadequacy. Gradually she was able to recognize and reveal her unsureness about herself in her role as a woman. She slowly abandoned her attitude of contempt for her mother as she began to recognize the envy that lay behind it. A rather revealing episode of the past was then brought out. Ruth told about a visit she had made to the home of a friend. While she was there a group of boys whom she had not known well, just returned from college, had come in. She had observed that the other girls enjoyed seeing the boys but she had felt isolated. Suddenly, during the interview, she burst into tears, saying "My father won't let me have a permanent." It then came out that, although Ruth's straight hair harmonized well with her features, she wanted a permanent wave. Her father appreciated the girl's classical beauty, brought out by her straight hair. He recognized that she had beauty that would be a real asset to a woman; he did not know that it was not the type that would be appealing to the high school age group. He had never let her have a permanent wave because to him it would look artificial. Outwardly she had accepted this attitude. The lack of a permanent wave had become to her a symbol, however, of her inadequacy as a woman. She was certain if she had curly hair the boys would like her. To her it was obvious that her father would not let her be attractive to other men but wanted her only for himself; that she would lose his affection completely if she interested other males.

Fortunately, the father was co-operative, and was willing, when the therapist suggested it, to let Ruth have a permanent wave. The result was a much less classical appearance in the girl; she looked like every other high school girl. The psychological metamorphosis in the girl was striking. She abandoned her rejection of the boys and girls of her own age and began to participate actively in their social life. Fortunately, the boys responded very readily to this change in her. She found that she enjoyed parties and that she was really more interested in the typical conversations of her own age group than she was in philosophical discussions with her father. She began to enjoy conversations with her mother, too, and commented that she was surprised to find that her mother really knew more about the world as it was lived day by day than her father did, in spite of his scholarly approach. Indicative of the change in this girl was her remark, "Gee, it is fun just to ride in a convertible with a bunch of kids making noise."

At no time in treatment was the classical picture of the "oedipal triangle" directly handled with Ruth. The goal of treatment was to help her direct her libidinal drives away from her father to her own age group. As this occurred, healthy defenses were developed against the pull toward her father. At the same time she was assisted in finding expression for normal feminine interests, not only in terms of her sublimated sexual drives but also in the non-sexual areas of femininity. Fortunately, this girl had not reached a stage in which she was able to defend herself too effectively against her wish to be a woman. That the treatment was not just verbally successful was indicated by the fact that her dysmenorrhea completely disappeared.

Whether this girl will go on to develop healthy sublimations and a non-neurotic character structure cannot be answered at this time. It is quite possible that the underlying problems in regard to her father remain unsolved and that at a subsequent date, in order for her to make a really satisfactory adjustment she will need more intensive insight therapy. In the meantime, however, she is developing an ego strength that will make that type of treatment a safe approach. It is questionable whether it would have been safe at the time that she originally came in for treatment.

Ann

Ann, age 15, presented a somewhat different problem. Her presenting symptom was severe diarrhea that kept her away from school and from social activities. Her mother came in first to see the therapist and gave the following history. Ann had adjusted very well until the onset of menstruation. Until that time she had led an active, normal social life, had been popular with girls and boys, and had done well academically. In contrast to her very difficult younger brother, she had never presented any problems of behavior at home. She tended to play a maternal role toward this younger brother. Shortly after her first menstrual period the diarrhea began. At about the same time her relationship with her own age group underwent a change. She began to refuse dates, claiming that she did not like boys. On the few dates that she did accept she was extremely unhappy. She was particularly concerned because the boys wanted to kiss her. She reacted to this with revulsion because she thought the mouth was dirty. She was particularly disturbed if the boy's lips were moist. She said that it made her feel as if he were smearing something all over her face.

Ann had given up all her contacts with girls with the exception of Betty. The mother did not understand why Ann liked Betty, who was so different from Ann. Betty probably was sexually promiscuous; at least she herself said she was. Ann and Betty spent many hours together. Betty dominated the conversation, telling of her various questionable exploits with boys. When Ann spoke of this girl she spoke of her with contempt, saying that she could not understand anyone's exposing herself to the type of experience Betty reported.

Another significant factor that aided in the understanding of the problem was the appearance of Ann's mother. She was extremely well dressed and looked like a young woman in her twenties. Although she had been married for many years she gave the impression of still seeking a "boy friend." There was no indication that this was acted out in any way except as a harmless flirtation. As far as could be determined during the entire process of treatment, the mother was technically loyal to her husband, a man for whom she had little regard since she felt that he was very inferior to her.

In appearance, Ann was an immature model of her mother. She had many possibilities of developing into a very attractive woman, but was self-conscious and awkward. As treatment developed, Ann gave a picture of the family life. Her father preferred her to the brother. This gave her little gratification because she shared the mother's contempt for the father's crudeness and lack of intellectual interests. Ann felt that she was very close to her mother. Frequently they were taken for sisters. She recognized that this mistake by other people infuriated her; she did not want an older sister, she wanted a mother. Ann told the therapist that whenever she had a date her mother always met the boy when he arrived. While Ann was getting her coat on the mother would carry on a very animated conversation with the boy. Frequently, in spite of previous plans to the contrary, Ann and her boy friend spent the evening at home talking to her mother. The boy would then comment that the mother was really more fun than a movie would have been; she was so charming, she was so easy to talk to, she was so interesting. In making future plans with Ann, the boy would want to include the mother. Often the three spent the evening at home. At first Ann spoke of this with great enthusiasm, saying that it was wonderful to have a mother who was so attractive to boys. Finally it became clear that Ann actually felt like a third person on such occasions. She was certain she could never successfully compete with her mother.

Ann later had a dream in which she was at a party where her mother was the belle of the ball. Ann ran into the bathroom because of severe gastrointestinal cramps. When she reached the bathroom she decided that if she could escape from the house she would be all right. She climbed out of the bathroom window and ran away. Her cramps stopped and the dream ended.

During this period of treatment Ann had also discussed her friendship with Betty. It became apparent that Betty represented what Ann really wanted to be, a person who was confident and free in her sexuality. Before Ann could wisely accept this freedom she needed help in establishing her own standards of behavior and her own goals for herself as a woman.

Because of the mother's need to compete with her daughter, it was impossible to find any solution for Ann in her own home situation. Not only did she feel she could not compete with her more sophisticated mother but, as she attempted to do so, the mother did everything to belittle Ann and place her in an awkward situation with the boys. The only solution for Ann was to do as she did in the dream—to get away from her mother. A co-educational boarding school proved a very happy and successful experience for her, with an immediate disappearance of her gastrointestinal symptoms. Only two days after her return home for her summer vacation, the physical symptoms returned with their previous severity. She recognized the significance of this and was fortunate enough to find immediate work as a counselor at a camp. The gastrointestinal symptoms disappeared.

In the next few years Ann developed tools for handling the situation and was finally able to be with her mother without a return of her physical illness. In this particular case, one of the aspects of the diarrhea was her association of sexuality with smearing. The diarrhea served as a substitute sexual outlet as well as an expression of her anger toward her mother. The secondary gain of the illness permitted her to regress to an infantile level with the mother, who gave her attention because she was sick. During treatment she gained no insight into the meaning of the diarrhea except for its value in holding her mother's attention.

Paul

Occasionally, in treatment of the adolescent, spectacular results are obtained by relatively simple interpretation. Paul was a 14-year-old boy who for two years had been dangerously ill with severe ulcerative colitis. He had been kept alive by repeated, frequent blood transfusions. He responded to no medical therapy directed toward the basic physical condition. As a last resort he was referred for psychiatric treatment. When he appeared at the therapist's office his condition was of such a nature that the therapist hesitated to treat him outside the hospital. He was so bloodless that his skin was transparent; his ears looked as if they were made of tissue paper; he was literally a structure of bones tightly covered by thin skin. Any movement resulted in severe shortness of breath and he was so weak he could scarcely talk. The referring physician refused to hospitalize him because he felt that the specialties in the medical profession, other than psychiatry, had done everything they could do. While it was dangerous to the boy not to have repeated blood transfusions, they were proving ineffectual. The internist felt that if psychotherapy did not prove helpful the boy was doomed to death within a few months at the most.

This boy was extremely inarticulate. Most of the history was obtained from his mother, who spoke practically no English. The significant history material obtained could be pieced together enough to give some picture of the child's early life. In contrast to several older brothers who had been rather aggressive and in conflict with the standards of the parents, this boy had always been docile. To the mother he had always been the perfect son. The onset of the ulcerative colitis had been sudden as far as could be determined. Apparently it had not been precipitated by any particular episode, but its beginning was coincident with the drafting into the army of his older brother, who had been the most obstreperous member of the family. The older brother had been glad to join the army because it gave him a reason for breaking completely with the family.

During the first interview, Paul responded to most questions monosyllabically. When the therapist commented that Paul must have found it disheartening to be ill for two years at a time when he probably was interested in the activities in which his friends were participating at school, he answered that he had not minded because he had kept up with his school work while in the hospital. The therapist, still attempting to break through his indifference, remarked that she understood that he had always been a very good boy and never appeared angry at anyone. She doubted that anyone went through life without sometimes becoming angry. He answered that he never had been angry. When he was asked if there was anything in the family situation that he had ever been unhappy about, he agreed that there was. He was upset because his brothers sometimes showed anger at his mother and father. The therapist commented that she thought this was normal on the part of his brothers; children did become angry at the restrictions parents imposed. This comment was met with apparently complete indifference by the boy.

Two days later Paul returned for a second hour. He said he had had a dream that frightened him. He had dreamed he was home and was standing in front of a closet door that was carefully closed. He heard a noise in the closet and a voice said, "Open the closet door." He was afraid to open it; he was certain the noises he heard were made by wild animals. If freed they would not only destroy him but also his sleeping family. The voice, however, was so insistent in its demand that he finally began to open the door. He awakened in terror. The therapist suggested that this dream seemed to be related to her comment during the last hour in which she pointed out to him that it was normal for children sometimes to be angry at their parents. He apparently felt that anger at the parents would result in releasing wild animals that would destroy everyone. This interpretation brought no comment.

The therapist's next attempt to do something for the boy led to a discussion with him of the possibility that he might have some social contact with other boys his own age. She suggested that there might be some program at the Y.M.C.A. in which he could participate which would be within his physical capacity and would give him some opportunity to join his own age group. He lethargically agreed that it might be worth trying. When the suggestion was made to the mother, the mother accepted it reluctantly, since she felt it was not safe for the boy ever to be away from her surveillance. Using the authority of the medical profession, the therapist persuaded the mother to allow the boy to go to the Y.M.C.A.

Because of the absence of the therapist, the next interview was two weeks later. Paul then spoke of his Y.M.C.A. activities with some pleasure, but he had decided that there really was not enough to do. It then came out that he was using the time when he was permitted by his mother to be at the Y.M.C.A. to walk a few blocks from the home to watch other boys play baseball. During the last few days the boys had invited him to join the game for a few minutes at a time. They agreed he could drop out of the game when it proved too physically exhausting. Again there was an interruption in treatment and he returned about a month later. At this time he admitted that, without his mother's knowledge, he was actively participating in the ball games in the neighborhood. He was also going to the beach to swim, an activity forbidden by the mother. He commented that he had not had any intestinal bleeding for a few days, the first time in two years that there had been a real cessation. From that time on the ulcerative colitis rapidly healed. Some five years later Paul was seen again by the therapist. He was a well-built, though somewhat slight person, his color was good; he had been pronounced cured by his internist.

It is difficult to explain such a spectacular cure. The most likely explanation would seem to be that this boy actually was struggling with a strong aggressive drive which he dared not express because it involved hostility toward a mother unoriented to American culture. The dream, which interestingly enough was the only dream the boy ever offered in the brief therapy period, would suggest that Paul saw his strong aggressive drive solely as a destructive force. Because this boy was psychologically amorphous at the time he came for treatment, the therapist probably became a substitute for the mother. In that role she gave the boy permission to strike out for himself, relieved him of guilt for such behavior by her implied permissiveness, and implicitly reassured him that his aggressiveness would not destroy either himself or his family. He found ways to express himself aggressively without the knowledge of his real mother. She became aware of his activities only after physical recovery had occurred. This boy had held himself in with a rigidity that was based upon panic. Once the panic was slightly relieved, the rigidity dissolved and he found acceptable outlets for his normal aggressiveness.

Goals in Treatment

In the treatment of adolescents, orientation to the dynamics of behavior is essential. In the author's opinion, however, this knowledge should be utilized not to give deep insight to the young adolescent, but rather to understand the forces to which the adolescent is exposed which have proved too great for his ego adaptation. In treating most young adolescents, the goal should be to give only sufficient insight to relieve the strain on the ego and, wherever possible, to lessen the external pressures that intensify the adolescent's problem. The aim of treatment should be primarily to protect the weakened ego in order to facilitate its convalescence. As the ego is strengthened, personality structuralization occurs. Ideally, one would wish the structuralization to be free of neurotic components; actually, this frequently will not be true. Once the structuralization does occur, however, the individual is then ready for deeper psychoanalytical therapy. Structuralization of the personality occurs as a result of the increased capacity of the ego to find some solution to the multiple problems that are pressing during the adolescent period.

When the ego of the adolescent has become stronger, and organized defenses are becoming apparent, although perhaps not yet completely established, the individual can profit from psychoanalytical therapy. In such treatment, however, the therapist needs to be extremely sensitive to the ego's tolerance for insight. Therapy with this age group, even more than with adults, is wise only if the treatment repeatedly supports the ego-adaptive aspects of the psychological structure while the individual gains insight into his unconscious motivations. In such treatment the therapist as a person is equally as important as the therapist as a transference figure. Psychoanalysis, even in modified form, is indicated, in the author's opinion, only toward the end of the adolescent period. The terminal period of adolescence, as has been pointed out repeatedly, is not measured by the individual's chronological age; it can be determined only by a careful study of his underlying problems and of the defenses that he is utilizing to deal with these underlying problems.

The treatment of choice for the individual adolescent is determined primarily by an evaluation of the present ego strength as well as of the ultimate ego potential. In the normal adolescent, the period of minimum ego strength is at the time when the impact of the psychological effect of the secretion of the reproductive organs is first experienced. The ego is temporarily severely crippled because of the multiple demands that are placed on it. Gradually it begins to show signs of recovery. Evidence of convalescence is often found in the beginning manifestations of consistently utilized defenses. Until these defenses have become relatively crystallized, treatment should foster the ego potentials and assist in developing as healthy defenses as are possible against the primitive expression of inherent impulses. Once the ego manifests increased strength to deal with the internal and external problems with consistent defenses, the patient can, if adequately supported in therapy, utilize insight. The result of this insight would be, it is hoped, the abandonment of unnecessary defenses and the constructive utilization of necessary defenses in the formulation of the total personality.

X. Sex Education and Sexual Behavior

During the past twenty-five years, increasing stress has been placed upon the value of wisely given sex information. Parents have been advised to answer the small child's questions frankly. The anticipation has been that in this way the child will not only gain factual knowledge but will also, in adulthood, accept his own sexuality rather than be frightened and confused by it. It is to be hoped that in the near future a critical study will be made of the end results of early sex education.

Clinically, it is interesting to observe how often a child who was given adequate sex information in early childhood later has "forgotten" much of it. If the facts have not been forgotten and even if they have been supplemented by studies in physiology and biology, the acceptance of the adult sexual role does not seem to be markedly facilitated. Frigidity and impotence continue to present a problem to many individuals. This is not surprising when one considers the fundamental difficulties involved in accepting sexuality. As one adolescent expressed it, "It is not the physiology and anatomy that we don't understand but rather our feelings. We want to know what they mean and what to do about them."

Group Discussions

With the well-meaning intention of easing the problem of sexual adjustment for the adolescent, high schools often welcome lecturers who will discuss with the young people not only the factual questions they may have in regard to sex but also their emotional difficulties in accepting sexuality. Many dangers are inherent in this plan. In a teen-age group great variation will exist in the nature of the individual conflicts. Some members of the group may be thrown into a state close to panic, of which they do not know the origin, and therefore may be unable to ask questions that would relieve the panic. Answers given to other questions may, as a result of an attempt to reconcile conscious concepts with unconscious conflicts, be misinterpreted and distorted. Quite possibly, for many youngsters the anxiety will be intensified rather than diminished.

The author has had opportunity to gather limited information on the effectiveness of group discussion of sexuality in a small number of cases, as well as to observe the deleterious effect of such discussions upon one individual of the group. A group of high school girls of average to superior intelligence was invited to attend three lectures on sex. In the first lecture the anatomy and physiology of the sexual function of the body were reviewed and a description of intercourse, pregnancy, and the birth process was given. The other two lectures were devoted to a discussion of the emotional problems of adolescent sexuality and the significance of characteristic behavior. The girls participated actively, raising questions and expressing their own attitudes. During the course of the two lectures the point was made that sexual feelings were normal but needed to be understood; that it was important for a girl not only to understand her feelings but to have a point of view that governed her expression of them. A considerable part of the discussion was concerned with dancing, hugging, and kissing. It was recognized that such activities drained off certain tensions but, if not wisely controlled, might also increase tension.

A few weeks after the completion of the series, fourteen of the girls were interviewed individually by the lecturer. Seven of them commented favorably on the meetings. They felt that the lecture on anatomy and physiology was not too important, since they did not care too much about how the body actually worked. Their real concern had been about their feelings. As a result of the discussion, they felt that they not only understood their feelings but that they had formulated a point of view that would have real influence on their actual behavior. These seven girls had come to the conclusion that their wish to have a sexual experience had been motivated more by curiosity than by a real sexual need. They had concluded that they would probably wait until marriage to experience intercourse; they would at least wait until they were older and were surer of their own goals. The other seven reacted quite in contrast. They stated either that they did not understand the lectures and the discussion or that they had forgotten what was discussed. With one exception, they denied any problem in their relationship with boys; they claimed rather that they were indifferent to boys.

The one exception said that the lectures had been disturbing to her. This particular girl was 17 years old, of very superior intelligence. She had given some evidence previously of being disturbed but not so seriously that the social worker who knew her had felt any real concern about her. The girl informed the lecturer that she did not believe the lecturer had told the truth. When questioned about the statements she thought had been false, she recalled that in the discussion most of the girls had indicated that discreet kissing and hugging were gratifying and acceptable behavior. She herself would never kiss a boy until she was married. The interviewer pointed out to her that one of the concepts that came out in the discussion was that each person would find a somewhat different answer to the question; the important goal was to find an answer that the individual really respected. The interviewer, however, commented that she would be interested in knowing why this girl had come to this particular decision about kissing. The girl stated then that she read widely, mentioning such magazines as *True Confessions*. She had noted in these stories frequently that shortly after the boy and girl had kissed, the girl became pregnant, with no mention of anything else happening in between. She was convinced, therefore, that it was erroneous to think that kissing would not result in pregnancy. This might have been offered only as a humorous example of a defense on the part of a young girl not ready yet to accept her own sexuality, had not the girl developed, about a month later, an acute psychotic episode. Under psychiatric treatment it became evident that, although underlying problems had weakened the girl's psychological health, a precipitating factor in the acute breakdown was the impact of the material to which she had been exposed in the discussion group.

Another group of somewhat more sophisticated girls invited a psychiatrist to conduct six meetings to discuss the questions they had concerning their sexual behavior. These girls were high school graduates and were employed. It was a homogeneous group to the extent that they shared most of their recreational activities The subjects for discussion were based upon the girls' own questions, which were submitted prior to the first meeting. Again the leader interpreted the emotional factors involved, with the group participating freely. At the end of the six meetings the members were asked to fill in, without signing, a questionnaire, the last query of which was, "Is there any question you feel was not answered in the discussion?" Actually, all the questionnaires were signed.

Tabulation of the answers showed a uniform enthusiasm about the meetings, with frequent comments indicating that each member felt the entire experience had been of great value in clarifying her thinking and her practical approach to her sexual problems. In view of the satisfactory comments, the answer to the last question was significant. Each person listed as unanswered the specific question that she had submitted. Subsequently, two of the group sought psychiatric treatment. It was interesting then to find that both again presented as their basic problem the same question they had raised in the discussion group. Very brief exploration made it clear that the question not only revealed, but at the same time masked, an underlying problem. The answers that were given were in a sense irrelevant because they did not dissolve the defenses or diminish the underlying confusion.

Were the defenses of the adolescent more adequate to deal with highly emotionally charged situations, group discussions would have many more advantages and fewer dangers. Adolescents do not have such serviceable defenses. It would appear wiser to discuss sexual problems individually. Under individual guidance it is easier to determine what information the person is actually seeking than can be done in a group situation, and evidence of disturbance over the material can be more readily recognized and handled. Problems revealed in the discussion can be related to the total problem of the individual. The manifest anxiety about sex may be only the shadow cast by a much broader problem.

Inevitably, when adolescents are together in a group, they will frequently discuss sex. If an adult is also present, the adult certainly should not show disapproval or fail to participate. If the discussion becomes prolonged, however, he should gradually direct the group to some other topic if for no other reason than to stimulate multiple interests. Whether the adult is participating in a discussion with an individual or a group, it is imperative that he be aware of his reasons for participating. To be helpful, he should not be motivated by the vicarious gratification gained through talking about what is frightening or forbidden, but by a mature wish to help the young persons clarify facts and feelings about sexuality.

Changing Mores

The responsibility assumed in helping an adolescent through the fog of his sexual confusion is not one to undertake lightly. Hidden by the fog are real as well as fantasied dangers. Which of the dangers are real and which are fantasied is not always clear to the adult any more than to the young person. Because our culture is not static and its social laws are not permanent, sexual mores are constantly undergoing change. Changes occur insidiously; it is difficult to say at what point they become incorporated into the true mores of the group. They originate probably in the neurotic needs of a few individuals but are later accepted for non-neurotic reasons by others. Every older generation shakes its collective head over the behavior of the younger generation. The older generation has always frowned upon the younger. Viewed in historical perspective, this attitude is amusing, but to be only amused is to risk overlooking the significance of this reaction. Measured by the older generation's standards, the younger generation is in danger. As young people violate established criteria for proper conduct, they may expose themselves to possible disastrous consequences. If, however, they find that the risks were exaggerated, they modify the codes of behavior which the older generation found constructive. The ultimate effect of this modification upon the individual and upon society cannot easily be ascertained. The older generation has some justification for viewing with alarm changes initiated by young people.

Persons working with adolescents face a dilemma. They can attempt to retard social change by guiding the individual along the familiar paths of the past. These paths may have limitations, but the limitations at least are known. They can, in contrast, accept changes in social conduct that may arise from the adolescent's confusion, his eagerness to find new ways of expression, his limited experiences, and his lack of perspective. These changes cannot be accurately evaluated until time has passed and the results can be observed.

No aspects of the evolving adaptive pattern of the adolescent is more challenging than that in the sexual sphere. Sexual customs seem always to have been in a state of flux. The twentieth century is not unique in this respect, but the changes of this century have most significant bearing on the present problems and the future adjustment of today's adolescent. The Puritan background of the American people demanded a strict prohibition of sexual gratification. Even as late as the beginning of this century, virginity and frigidity in woman were considered by many to be evidence of her superiority to the animal nature of man. Not many years ago a girl felt she lost her purity—symbolically, her virginity—if she allowed a boy to kiss her. Most girls undoubtedly sacrificed their purity but did so feeling guilty. Overt changes in sexual behavior and attitudes accompanied the social upheavals of the first World War. Sex was something to flaunt. The biological urge was exposed in its nudity. In fear of being branded sentimental, the emotional overtones of love were hidden from view. It is likely that most young people secretly enriched the biological activity by allowing themselves to experience the emotional overtones, but kept their tender feeling concealed from public view. Out of this background a new sexual pattern seems to be evolving, the end results of which cannot yet be forecast.

Even though we recognize that the older generation again is seeing the behavior of the younger generation through jaundiced eyes, it is probable that, at the present time, greater sexual freedom exists among young people than was true in the not too distant past. Certainly "necking" is engaged in more openly than it was formerly. Mutual genital stimulation, while not accepted as casually as necking, has a recognized place in the development of a close relationship. Intercourse prior to marriage is accepted as a natural part of the courtship by a large percentage of the young group.

It is often difficult to evaluate the significance of any one individual's sexual behavior in the light of the changing social patterns. There is no question but that many girls and boys become prematurely involved in sexual activities before they have reached a psychological maturity that is an inherent part of true heterosexual adjustment. Many of them are acting out problems related to feelings of inadequacy or to infantile neuroses. In such instances the sexual behavior is pre-heterosexual or distorted heterosexuality, and is utilized as an attempt to solve previously unsolved difficulties. On the other hand, with a more permissive attitude toward sex it is not surprising if young people who reach the point of emotional maturity compatible with heterosexuality find a direct expression for their sexual urge rather than being pressed into either repression or sublimation of the drive.

The first step in a diagnostic appraisal of an individual's sexual behavior is to determine whether he is expressing neurotic or mature drives in his behavior. Although this discussion is focused upon the adolescent, the same diagnostic challenge faces persons dealing with any biologically sexual individual, whether that individual is 17 or 50, single or married.

A definition of true heterosexual maturity is not easy to formulate. From one standpoint it is the development of the biologically determined, although psychologically colored, capacity for genital response. Over and above this, however, it is related to the general emotional maturity of the individual. Dr. Leon J. Saul states, "The mature attitude toward sexuality seems to be little different from a mature attitude toward work or toward social living. When the sexuality and the rest of the personality mature together, the two are integrated in a proper balancing of the needs for love, the self-love and the self-interest with a high degree of enjoyment of the loving, activity, interest and responsibility involved in the relationship to lover, work and friends." [1] Again he points out that sexual maturity "is characterized by independence, produc-

[1] Leon J. Saul, M.D., *Emotional Maturity*, J. B. Lippincott Company, Philadelphia, 1947, 13.

tivity, and 'object interest' in the sexual as well as in the social spheres." [2] In other words, mature heterosexual love is broader than simply the capacity to respond physically to sexual experiences. It encompasses the total personality, and is an expression of an enriched capacity to give as well as to receive love. By these criteria, sexual promiscuity leading to physical gratification without the enrichment that a meaningful relationship with the love object contributes is not an expression of sexual maturity.

Whether, if culturally accepted, sexual promiscuity in adolescents —because of the sexual experience itself—can be a step toward true sexual maturity is a question that can only be answered speculatively at the present time. The long existence of a "double standard" in our culture seems at least to show that, except when other factors exist, sexual promiscuity has not distorted the ultimate pattern of maturity in men. A single standard with acceptance of early sexual experiences may not per se be deleterious. The concept of the "double standard," however, contained certain psychological implications that make it different from the question of general sexual freedom. The boy's early sexual initiation was with a depreciated woman. As he attained true maturity, and married, he chose a love object with whom he could gratify biological sexuality, with the added overtones of a fused sexual and asexual love. Whether the new pattern, which does not separate sexual from sentimental love, creates serious psychological problems can only be speculated upon at the present time. The study of mores of other cultures also cannot supply definitive answers to the various questions. An appraisal of the risks and values must be based on careful study of the end results of greater sexual freedom in this particular culture.

If the end results of the present trend cannot be predicted, certain steps at least can be taken to minimize possible unfortunate effects. Since sexual maturation is a significant component of psychological growth, any aid that can be given to facilitate healthy psychological growth will have direct bearing on the ease with which sexual maturity can be reached. Sexual maturation also will be aided by the reduction of sexual confusion. The adolescent will be less frightened by the conflicting impulses he experiences if he feels

[2] *Ibid.*, 126.

that he has genuine support from those who have gained some security in an adult world. As the adolescent gradually formulates his own philosophy and standards, he will develop a standard about sexual conduct. He can be helped to clarify his attitudes about various life problems by wise and flexible guidance. As has been stressed earlier, guidance should not be confused with rigid dictatorial control.

The adolescent also needs to be aware of the reality aspects of sexuality. The reality is not limited to the danger of pregnancy and venereal disease. Contraceptive methods have been perfected so that at the present time pregnancy need not be a consequence of intercourse. The danger of the spread of venereal in infection is minimal if sexual experiences are limited to those with others of the same social group. More significant psychological problems develop if the individual acts on impulse rather than within the framework of his philosophy—a philosophy formulated during a time when he can be more objective because he is less pressed by impulses demanding expression. Impulsive behavior that violates basic attitudes leads to overwhelming guilt. A safeguard to fundamental emotional peace is a philosophy vital enough to inhibit a response to momentary stimulation which would lead to behavior unacceptable to the self.

Complications in adjustment which seem to result from the acceptance of a change in sexual mores may not be entirely attributable to the undesirability of the new patterns. Some of the unfortunate results may be only a reflection of a more general psychological disturbance in a particular individual. Some general problems or ramifications of them may develop with a frequency that suggests wide or universal negative effects of the external pattern on psychological development. Many girls, for example, although they appear to accept the attitude of their peers that intercourse prior to marriage is a natural phase of growing up, find they are frigid. In some cases the frigidity is due to conflicts that would be equally powerful in marriage; they would be frigid whether they were married or not. In our present culture, however, female sexuality is closely tied to the emotional implication of a home and motherhood. The absence of these components in the immediate relationship may result in sexual inhibition and frigidity. The frigidity frightens the girl, making her feel that she is sexually inadequate. Secondary problems may be created which would not have been present had the sexual experience been in the framework of marriage.

Even though the peer group may accept greater sexual freedom, the parental group on the whole does not. One occasionally sees a girl who has been away from the direct influence of home and has been a member of a group that accepts direct sexual expression. While with the group the girl has no particular conflict about her own behavior. She lives in a world from which her parents are not only physically but also emotionally absent. Some difficulty arises that causes her to return to her parents. She may be struggling with an emotionally charged problem that she cannot solve. She may wish to return—emotionally if not physically—to her parents for the support she needs, which the peer group does not offer and which the parents in the past have provided. Parental attitudes again become significant to her. Guilt over her violation of parental standards—a guilt that had been kept in check or alleviated by the support of the peer group—now becomes overwhelming. Needing her parents, she fears that she will lose their support because of her failure to live up to their standards. Because now her parents are needed more than the peer group is, she becomes acutely disturbed over her past.

One girl described her feeling by saying, "My sexual life seemed so beautiful while I was living it. Now that I have come home I feel soiled." While such a reaction is obviously indicative of emotional immaturity with the resultant absence of a comprehensive philosophy of her own, it is not a surprising reaction in a girl who has not yet had time to reach real emotional adulthood. The attitude she expressed is a specific example of the general confusion of the adolescent in his attempt to revolt against his infantile superego and to construct a mature superego. His abandonment of the infantile superego frightens him if his own internal support fails him and he wishes to supplement it by returning to a dependent relationship with parental figures. He fears he has lost, and often has lost, external parental protection before his own strengths are adequately developed. Even though one believes that a mature individual can have sexual gratification on a heterosexual level without guilt prior to marriage, it is not necessarily true that the adolescent in his confusion can do likewise.

In summary, it should be recognized that young people today—as every group of young people has done throughout history—are abandoning certain standards previously established by parental figures and are struggling to establish a new approach to life. We cannot help them by rigidly imposing a code of behavior that will bind them to the past, unless we wish to deprive our culture of the opportunity for progressive enrichment. On the other hand, we cannot expect confused, inexperienced, and frightened adolescents to build a new world alone. We need to recognize that changes will occur, that these changes will be more likely to evolve constructively if we offer wise support and honest presentation of our limited knowledge. The adolescent should have a reason to believe that we respect ourselves, and that we also respect him. He has a right to expect us to have confidence not only in our own attitudes but also in his ability to find a valid philosophy for himself. He should have evidence that, whenever possible, we will help him. We should attempt to protect him wisely and to give him sufficient freedom to facilitate his maturation. Above all, we must give him time to draw up his blueprints for his adult world. We cannot, if we wish to aid him, treat him as a child, but it is equally true that we cannot demand that he be an adult.

XI. Conclusions

ADOLESCENCE IS A STAGE of emotional growth. It cannot be avoided if adulthood is to be attained. It is a period in which many conflicts dormant since childhood return to be solved. It is a period also of new problems, problems created by the physical changes that have occurred in the individual.

The psychological structure of the adolescent has much in common with a jig-saw puzzle. Early adolescence corresponds to the time when the pieces of the jig-saw puzzle lie chaotically in a heap with no part fitted to another. As the reconstruction of the picture is undertaken, one piece is found to fit another. Several groups of three or four pieces then are joined together but their relationship to the total picture is still obscure. Ultimately these nuclei can be interlocked with others and finally the total picture is produced. The adolescent, in the same way, finds patterns for joining small sections of his feelings together, finally combining all the islands of adjustment into a completed picture—his adult personality.

During the early part of adolescence the pressures from physical, psychological, and social changes are of such intensity that the adaptive capacity of the individual is strained to the point of relative inadequacy. During the period of rapid physical development the lack of physical stability adds to the strain. When physical maturation is relatively complete the strain lessens. Physical functioning of the body becomes more uniform. It is easier to adapt to a constant factor than a fluctuating one. In effect, once the physical structure is somewhat stabilized the individual has an opportunity to become familiar with it and this familiarity results in progressive mastery. In a like manner, familiarity with the social demands and the psychological pressures clarifies the issues and facilitates their mastery. Until this stabilization and clarification have been achieved, the individual has no real foundation upon which to build an adult personality structure. When the foundation is laid, he can deal in a more orderly fashion with those psychological problems that relate to his early experiences, to his early defenses, and to his drive toward integrated maturation.

To return to the analogy of the jig-saw puzzle, the stabilization and clarification are comparable to the peripheral frame of the finished picture. Many people attack the problem of putting the separate parts of the puzzle together in an orderly fashion; they first piece together the frame and gradually build in until the isolated fragments can be put together to make the total picture. The frame gives a point of reference for the location of the other parts.

If, while a jig-saw puzzle is being put together, pieces are pushed off the table or pieces that have been sorted out are again mixed with unrelated ones, the process is more complicated, and the completion of the task delayed. Similarly, adolescence is delayed when external situations disrupt the organizing process. Just as, at times, pieces of a jig-saw puzzle are lost and the picture never reaches completion, many adults do not quite complete the process of maturation. The gaps in integration—the neuroses of adulthood—are often created in adolescence and may never be filled in at all, or only after prolonged seeking with the aid of psychiatric techniques. Dynamic treatment attempts to place properly those pieces that were unrecognized or to find the pieces that were lost.

Many adolescents "live through" adolescence without any conscious planning or assistance from others. Some have the advantage of living in a milieu that is inherently helpful; others have more consciously planned assistance. Regardless of whether the adolescent is struggling through his problems alone or is aided in his adjustment by means of group activities, close personal relationships, environmental manipulation through guidance to the parents and the school, or whether he is receiving supportive or insight therapy, one generalization has validity: adolescence is a stage of emotional growth. It cannot be avoided if adulthood is to be attained. It may be prolonged because the individual is unable to find either a healthy or a neurotic solution to his conflicts. On the other hand, adolescence cannot be too greatly foreshortened without serious adverse effects. The normal adolescent needs time to grow up. He needs support, encouragement, and guidance, and, above all, adequate time before he is forced to crystallize his final personality pattern. Treatment, of whatever nature, should be geared to helping him utilize the adolescent period optimally. It should never have as its goal the avoidance of adolescence or the precipitous abandonment of it through a regression to childhood or to a pseudo-maturation emulating adulthood.

REFERENCES

PHYSICAL ASPECTS OF ADOLESCENCE

"Adolescence," *Forty-third Yearbook*, Part 1, National Society for the Study of Education, Chicago, 1944.

BROOKS, FOWLER, D.: *The Psychology of Adolescence*, Houghton Mifflin Co., Boston, 1929.

GREULICH, WILLIAM W.: "Some Observations on the Growth and Development of Adolescent Children," *Journal of Pediatrics*, XIX (1941), 302–314.

JOHNSTON, J. A.: "Nutritional Requirement of the Adolescent and Its Relation to the Development of Disease," *American Journal of Diseases of Children*, LXXIV (1947), 487–494.

PRATT, J. P.: "Endocrine Aspects of Adolescence," *American Journal of Diseases of Children*, LXXIV (1947), 507–513.

SHUTTLEWORTH, FRANK K.: *The Adolescent Period: A Graphic Atlas*, Child Development Publications of the Society for Research in Child Development, Northwestern University, Evanston, Illinois, 1951.

———: *The Adolescent Period: A Pictorial Atlas*, Child Development Publications of the Society for Research in Child Development, Northwestern University, Evanston, Illinois, 1951.

STUART, HAROLD C.: "Normal Growth and Development During Adolescence," *New England Journal of Medicine*, 234 (1946), 666–672, 693–700, 732–738.

———: "Physical Growth During Adolescence," *American Journal of Diseases of Children*, LXXIV (1947), 495–502.

SWEET, CLIFFORD D.: "Improvement of Body Mechanics in Adolescent Children," *American Journal of Diseases of Children*, LXXIV (1947), 503–506.

Symposium on Adolescence, *Journal of Pediatrics*, XIX (1941), 289–402.

WAISMAN, HARRY A., RICHMOND, JULIUS B., AND WILLIAMS, STARKS J.: "Vitamin Requirements in Adolescence," *Journal of Pediatrics*, XXXVII (1950), 922–935.

GENERAL REFERENCES ON ADOLESCENCE

"Adolescence," *Forty-third Yearbook*, Part 1, National Society for the Study of Education, Chicago, 1944.

AICHHORN, AUGUST: *Wayward Youth*, Viking Press, New York, 1935.

ARLOW, JACOB A.: "A Psychoanalytic Study of a Religious Initiation Rite, Bar Mitzvah," *The Psychoanalytic Study of the Child*, Vol. VI, International Universities Press, New York, 1951, 353–374.

AXELROD, PEARL L., CAMERON, MYRNA S., AND SOLOMON, JOSEPH C.: "An Experiment in Group Therapy with Shy Adolescent Girls," *American Journal of Orthopsychiatry*, XIV (1944), 616–627.

BERES, DAVID, AND OBERS, SAMUEL J.: "The Effects of Extreme Deprivation in Infancy on Psychic Structure in Adolescence," *The Psychoanalytic Study of the Child*, Vol. V, International Universities Press, New York, 1950, 212–235.

BERNFELD, S.: "Types of Adolescence," *Psychoanalytic Quarterly*, VII (1938), 243–253.

BLANCHARD, PHYLLIS: "Adolescent Experience in Relation to Personality and Behavior," *Personality and the Behavior Disorders* (J. McV. Hunt, editor), Vol. II, The Ronald Press, New York, 1944, 691–713.

BLOS, PETER: *The Adolescent Personality*, Appleton-Century, New York, 1941.
———: "The Essence of Adolescent Change," *Child Study*, XXIV (1947), 43–45, 62–63.
BORNSTEIN, BERTA: "On Latency," *The Psychoanalytic Study of the Child*, Vol. VI, International Universities Press, New York, 1951, 279–285.
BROOKS, FOWLER D.: *The Psychology of Adolescence*, Houghton Mifflin Co., Boston, 1929.
DEUTSCH, HELENE: *The Psychology of Women*, Vol. I, Grune & Stratton, New York, 1944.
FREUD, ANNA: *The Ego and the Mechanisms of Defence*, Hogarth Press, London, 1937.
GITELSON, MAXWELL: "Character Synthesis: The Psychotherapeutic Problem of Adolescence," *American Journal of Orthopsychiatry*, XVIII (1948), 422–431.
———: "Direct Psychotherapy in Adolescence," *American Journal of Orthopsychiatry*, XII (1942), 1–25.
HACKER, FREDERICK J., AND GELEERD, ELISABETH R.: "Freedom and Authority in Adolescence," *American Journal of Orthopsychiatry*, XV (1945), 621–630.
JOHNSON, ADELAIDE M.: "Sanctions for Superego Lacunae of Adolescents," *Searchlights on Delinquency* (K. R. Eissler, editor), International Universities Press, New York, 1949, 225–245.
——— AND FISHBACK, DORA: "Analysis of a Disturbed Adolescent Girl and Collaborative Psychiatric Treatment of the Mother," *American Journal of Orthopsychiatry*, XIV (1944), 195–203.
LANDER, JOSEPH: "The Pubertal Struggle Against the Instincts," *American Journal of Orthopsychiatry*, XII (1942), 456–461.
MEAD, MARGARET: *From the South Seas. Studies of Adolescence and Sex in Primitive Societies*, Wm. Morrow & Co., New York, 1939.
RALL, MARY E.: "Dependency and the Adolescent," *Journal of Social Casework*, XXVIII (1947), 123–130.
ROSS, HELEN: "The Case Worker and the Adolescent," *The Family*, XXII (1941), 231–238.
SCHMIDEBERG, MELITTA: "The Psycho-Analysis of Asocial Children and Adolescents," *International Journal of Psycho-Analysis*, XVI (1935), 22–48.
SPIEGEL, LEO A.: "A Review of Contributions to a Psychoanalytic Theory of Adolescence," *The Psychoanalytic Study of the Child*, Vol. VI, International Universities Press, New York, 1951, 375–393.
SYMONDS, PERCIVAL M.: *Adolescent Fantasy*, Columbia University Press, New York, 1949.
Symposium on Adolescence, *Journal of Pediatrics*, XIX (1941), 289–402.
TRYON, CAROLINE MCCANN: "Evaluations of Adolescent Personality by Adolescents," *Child Behavior and Development* (Roger G. Barker et al., editors), McGraw-Hill Book Co., New York, 1943, Chap. XXXI, 545–566.
WITTELS, FRITZ: "The Ego of the Adolescent," *Searchlights on Delinquency* (K. R. Eissler, editor), International Universities Press, New York, 1949.
YOUNG, LEONTINE R.: *The Treatment of Adolescent Girls in an Institution*, Child Welfare League of America, New York, 1945.
ZACHRY, CAROLINE, AND LIGHTY, MARGARET: *Emotion and Conduct in Adolescence*, Appleton-Century, New York, 1940.